KENNEL BUILDING AND MANAGEMENT

Kennel Building and Management

by

MARIO MIGLIORINI

HOWELL
BOOK HOUSE
New York

Howell Book House
Macmillan Publishing Company
866 Third Avenue, New York, NY 10022
Collier Macmillan Canada, Inc.

Library of Congress Cataloging-in-Publication Data
Migliorini, Mario.
  Kennel building and management.

  1. Kennels.   2. Kennel management.   I. Title.
SF428.M54   1987   636.7'01   87-21435
ISBN 0-87605-656-7

Some of the subject matter in this book first appeared as
articles in *Groomers' Gazette/Kennel News*.

Macmillan books are available at special discounts for bulk purchases
for sales promotions, premiums, fund-raising, or educational use.
For details, contact:

Special Sales Director
Macmillan Publishing Company
866 Third Avenue
New York, NY 10022

10 9 8 7

Printed in the United States of America

Contents

Profile of the Author   9

Foreword   11

1. Boarding Kennels: An Overview   15

Practical Design / Monitoring Boarders / Working with the Plant / How Infection Can Happen

2. One-Stop Pet Care   26

The Automation Concept / Boarding Kennels and Veterinarians / Total Pet Care Contract

3. Hobby Kennels   30

Kennel as Part of Home / Designing Your Own System / Additional Modifications / Run Surfaces

4. Care and Feeding Methods   44

Dealing with Stress / The Well-Adjusted Boarder / Handle with Caution / Exercise for Boarders / Which Diet Is Best?

5. Problem Dogs   51

Personality Types / Handling Unfriendly Dogs / A Sobering Case History

6. Handling Large Breeds   58

7. There's More Than One Way to Board a Cat   60

Housing Systems / Feeding and Sanitation / Health Questions / Handling / Odor Control

8. **Peak Boarding Management**   66

Reservation System

9. **The Formula for Success**   69

10. **Who's the Boss?**   72

The Client Calls the Shots / Why They Need You / Know Your Customers

11. **Making the Right Impression**   77

Your Business Name / Advertising / Your Telephone Manner / Your Personal Impression / Enhancing Your Business Image

12. **Good Public Relations**   83

Getting Customers' Confidence / Special Promotions / "Free" Advertising

13. **What's Your Sign?**   90

The Effective Sign / Cost and Impact

14. **Paying Your Way**   93

The Wise Uses of Credit / Obtaining Credit / Gross Income and Net Profit / Is There a Profit? / Is the Profit Sufficient? / Profit Trend

15. **Expand Your Business, Not Your Facility**   100

Promotion / Using the Media / Telling Your Story

16. **Capitalize on Impulse Buying**   104

Creative Merchandising / Effective Displays / Subletting Selling Space

17. **Kennel Computers**   109

Programs for Kennels / Essential Information

18. **Bad Checks Can Be "Made Good"**   111

When a Check Bounces / Protecting Yourself / When It Happens to You

19. **Infectious Diseases**   115

Canine Distemper / Hardpad / Infectious Hepatitis / Leptospirosis / Parvovirus / Coronavirus / Rabies / Canine Cough (Tracheobronchitis) / Brucellosis / Examining New Arrivals

20. **Controlling Pests and Parasites**   119

Flies / Mosquitoes / Fleas / Ticks / Cockroaches / Rats and Mice / Internal Parasites / Types of Parasites and Parasitism / Kennel Sanitation

21. Mange and Other Skin Disorders   126

Types of Mange / Skin Disorders

22. Allergies to Dogs and Cats   129

23. Diseases Communicable from Dog to Man   131

The Need for Caution / An Actual Case History

24. The Public's Attitude Toward Animals   138

Survey Findings / Benefits of Companion Animals / Attitudes Defined

25. Your Nose Knows   144

26. What Makes Good Kennel Help?   146

27. How Safe Is Your Kennel?   149

Electrical Circuits / Cages / Security / Self-Protection / General Conditions

28. Law Suits Over Dogs   155

Burden v. Hornsby (Old Drum), 1869 / Caswell v. Swavola / Other Legal Actions and Opinions / Legal Ramifications of Pet Owners Assisting Groomers

29. How to Live with the Law   163

Your Lawyer's Value to You / Legal Guidance in Organizing a Business / Legal Guidance in Acquiring Property / Buying Goods for Resale / Employees / Litigation / Handling Debt / Selling the Business

30. Self-Employment Standards for Groomers and Kennel Owners   167

Appendix

Innovative Kennels   175

The Monolithic Dome / Kennelwood Village / Preston Country Club for Pets

Kennel Plans   181
Sample Boarding and Grooming Contracts   191
Helpful Kennel Items   195

Profile of the Author

U NLIKE THOSE who apparently believe they can learn all about the pet care industry by osmosis, Mario Migliorini has served an extensive apprenticeship dating back to his childhood.

The son of a successful breeder and trainer of racing Greyhounds (who also kept and trained English Springer Spaniels and Labrador Retrievers for hunting), Mario by age 16 owned several winning Greyhounds he had raised and trained himself.

Mario also worked with the field dogs and learned the art of Wire Fox Terrier grooming from a family friend. He became seriously involved in breeding, training and showing Dobermans in obedience and conformation by the 1950s. He bred his first champion in 1955 and subsequently won many awards, including three Bests in Show, before turning professional.

During the late 1950s Mario was manager and handler for what was then one of the world's largest and most influential Poodle kennels. There he mastered the finer points of grooming Poodles, before moving on to a successful career as an AKC licensed all-breed handler.

In 1960, Mario Migliorini wrote a number of probing articles exploring the implications of hip dysplasia in Great Danes, helping to focus attention on this newly emerging problem at a time when little or no relevant information was available on the subject.

By 1961 Mario was operating one of the first full-service pet-care facilities in the country. It offered boarding for 170 animals; veterinary care; pet and show grooming; show handling, training and conditioning; handling classes; group and individual obedience training; security and guard dog training; field training; behavior modification; breeding and whelping services; dog importing and shipping; merchandising; selected puppy sales; and development and implementation of breeding programs for selected clients.

Plans for developing an even more elaborate facility were abandoned due to persistent health problems that eventually forced Mario to retire from professional handling.

Over the years Mario and his wife Margaret bred and owned a variety of dogs, many of them champions, including Dobermans, Greyhounds, Whippets, Springers, Cockers, Shelties, Miniature and Standard Schnauzers, Fox Terriers, Airedales, Poodles, Bull Terriers, Bulldogs, Afghans, Pekingese, Basenji, Pointers, Setters, Cairns, Westies, Pembroke Welsh Corgis, Great Danes, Labs, Alaskan Malamutes, German Shorthaired Pointers, German Shepherds, Brittanies, Weimaraners, Dalmatians and Spinoni Italianis.

Foreword

I CANNOT RECALL a time when my family did not own at least one dog and a cat or two. As a matter of fact, an old alley cat I found as a kitten when I was five years old lived with us for 18 years.

Looking back over the past 50 years it is clear that the general attitude toward animals has undergone many drastic changes. Companion animals have become part of the family to whom they belong and are not just possessions. Gone are the days when pets might be referred to as "worthless brutes," as once described in British law. Therefore, those who choose to care for other people's dogs and cats must be sure that these animals are housed in a suitable facility where they will remain safe and healthy.

I remember an occasion, when I was still in my preteens, when my father found it necessary to board two of his racing Greyhounds at a local kennel. While I don't recall all the details, I do remember that the dogs came home in terrible condition: undernourished, intimidated and infested with fleas.

Years later while exploring the possibility of buying kennel property I came across this same boarding kennel. It had been abandoned for years and was standing derelict.

The dogs, it seems, had been housed in a huge barn that had once been a stable. Around the walls were continuous benches made of rough-hewn oak, about 18 inches high and 24 inches wide. Heavy chains in three- to four-foot lengths were attached to the benches at regular intervals. Boarders were attached to these chains more or less at random. Straw was used on the benches as bedding and dogs who didn't like that had the option of sleeping on the cold, hard cobblestones that covered the floor.

11

Food and water was supplied in communal troughs. I hate to imagine the scene at mealtimes. The most commonly used dog food was stale wheat bread soaked in water, supplemented with stewed cow and hog lungs, cow's feet and offal acquired from the local slaughterhouse. Fortunately things have improved quite a bit in recent times. Obviously, that would not be too difficult!

In the early 1960s, daily boarding charges for an average-size dog were $1.50 to $2.00. Today it's $5.00 to $7.00 for a small dog or cat and may exceed $12.00 per day for large and giant breeds.

When I was actively involved in the pet-care business we had excellent facilities for about 175 animals. The main unit was newly built at a cost of $30,000. The value of the property, including an older dwelling, was approximately $100,000. Recently I received a circular offering a kennel for sale in California for $225,000. It was licensed for 60 dogs and cats, with only 17 runs of various sizes, but with room for expansion. However, the lot size was only 65 ft. × 150 ft., which included a four-bedroom home. Call it inflation.

My friends, most of whom had mastered the art of basic math, were readily able to compute that the income from the kennel could exceed $300 per day. Or, more impressively, $2,100 per week. Advanced mathematicians may have gone so far as to note that this income parlayed to more than $100,000 annually—not counting the possible related income from merchanising, training, handling, grooming and other services. They thought it was money for old rope!

Naturally my friends neglected to subtract net from gross: the cost of hiring competent help and other basic overheads like the monthly mortgage, heating, lighting, air conditioning, feed bills, general maintenance and repairs. That whittled down the profits alarmingly.

Most everyone believes that boarding fees are payment for purely custodial services. Unfortunately, it's not quite that uncomplicated. Anyone boarding dogs and cats has more to do than simply store the animal for a given period. The kennel operator is expected to return the dog or cat to its owner in optimum condition at the end of its stay. That may sound easy enough, but unfortunately we cannot warehouse animals in a convenient state of suspended animation. This makes pet care a potentially hazardous venture and by no means the easy money that some assume it to be.

Most owners believe their pets epitomize the well-mannered, cultured canine or feline. Maybe they do—at home. In the kennel they sometimes do an abrupt about-face and become willful, destructive and occasionally downright dangerous.

One of the most disconcerting and frustrating problems for the kennel operator is the perpetual escapee. Some animals seem to spend the entire visit trying to engineer a breakout. If they are once successful they become

12

obsessed with getting away as often as they possibly can. Losing a dog can be a worrisome and costly business, especially if escape is not covered by your insurance policy. Even when it is, the insurance company does not compensate for the unpleasantness or stress caused by the situation.

In a landmark decision several years ago, a California court awarded $1,000 to the owner of a stray kitten that got lost during its stay for a routine checkup at an animal hospital. The judgment was made against the veterinarian to whom the kitten was entrusted after being found abandoned on the plaintiff's doorstep. A similar kitten could have been obtained from any animal shelter for a few dollars. But the court upheld the owner's claim that the unfortunate incident had caused her young daughter great emotional trauma.

The potential for injury is another problem. Certain animals have a capacity to injure themselves through their own devices. While the dog or cat owner must theoretically prove negligence on the part of the kennel owner or members of the staff, in actuality it is the kennel owner who must establish innocence. Sometimes that is almost an impossible task. Even when one is successful, the legal costs and bad publicity can make it a hollow victory.

The responsibility one assumes while caring for other people's pets is more involved than locking them in a pen. Various sicknesses—canine cough, parvovirus, coronavirus, distemper, along with flea and tick infestations—may occur sporadically, regardless of the care you take. It's a big responsibility to undertake unless you are going to be sufficiently well paid for your efforts.

How well you do depends on several variables. However, having a well-designed facility that is managed correctly is a step in the right direction.

The purpose of this book is to outline proven methods used by some of the leaders in the field of kennel construction and management—both as a business and a hobby—that will make the reader aware of existing problems and possible solutions to them. This book is designed to provide current information about a variety of subjects relating to the operation of kennel establishments and is sold with the understanding that the author and publisher are not engaged in rendering legal, medical, accounting or other professional services. If legal, medical or other expert services are required, consult a qualified professional in your area.

1

Boarding Kennels: An Overview

W HILE REVIEWING THE variety of boarding and hobby kennels I've seen around the country (apart from the layout of the support areas: reception rooms, offices, kitchens, storage—features often governed by the size, shape and location of the lot), I found that basic kennel designs were remarkably similar. Most differences involved modifications made in adapting to the local climate or other variables existing in one area of the country and not another. There was a diversity of building materials used, but concrete block was by far the most popular.

Practical Design

Surprisingly, in most instances the design and construction of the kennel itself seemed to have received only secondary consideration to the esthetics of the accompanying housing accommodation. Most kennel owners, or perhaps I should say kennel builders, were apparently more concerned with the quality and comfort of the human living space than in an ultraefficient, functional kennel design. Most of the differences I saw were in the facades. With the average selling price of kennel property today estimated to be in the $300,000 range, it is understandable that buyers also want a nice home for that kind of money.

My main criticism is that 90 percent or more of today's kennel designs have totally inadequate provisions for the kennel owner's number-one operating problem: sanitation and waste disposal.

Most older commercial kenneling, like this training facility, was designed to function as a dog storage unit. While some facilities are more elaborate than others, the basic design is an inside pen connected to an outside run by a pophole. These units are generally stark, unimaginative and inefficient to operate.

Having low, wire-covered inside pens may save on the cost of initial construction, but this condemns the cleaning and maintenance person to hunching down and ducking in and out of them forever. Four-foot-high pens make cleaning operations tedious and inefficient and unless the kennel staff is very conscientious such conditions may ultimately contribute to neglected dogs and a rundown facility.

16

This is a more elaborate version of the typical indoor setup, but it still has similar drawbacks.

Heavy-duty, premium quality material is essential for commercial units. Note the way this lightweight wire has been abused by unwilling guests.

This kennel has dual popholes in each run. This permits twice the number of dogs to be exercised by rotating them throughout the day. Naturally, only one dog at a time is allowed in the run.

17

One hundred or more dogs in a confined space produce a substantial volume of excreta. The bigger the dogs, the bigger the problem. In most cases the architects seemed oblivious to this basic reality of animal husbandry. A large boarding kennel will generate over 50 tons of raw waste annually. Having once managed a Great Dane kennel with only minimum sanitation facilities, I guarantee it can make daily chores needlessly complicated and unpleasant for the cleanup crew. While not a popular topic of conversation in genteel company, it certainly needs to be addressed more realistically in the future than it has in the past.

An assortment of ultramodern designs have been proposed over the years. As far as I know none have yet come to fruition. In contrast, the reliable indoor/outdoor run concept has withstood the test of time remarkably well. While certainly not foolproof, it remains the most convenient and adaptable form of pet housing yet devised for confining a substantial number of dogs (and cats) under relatively safe conditions.

Personally, I do not favor giving dogs the option of going in and out at will. Having dealt with other people's animals for over thirty years, I am pessimistic about their propensity for self-destruction, and believe controlled, supervised exercise is a safer alternative. Left to their own devices, dogs usually manage to do something unexpected. As responsibility for what happens to kennel residents rests squarely with the kennel operator, there is no percentage in looking for trouble.

New arrivals are the main cause for concern and should be kept under observation until they have fully adjusted to their new surrounding and you are reasonably sure they are not potential candidates for committing hara-kiri while in your custody. I like the idea of using closed-circuit TV monitors to see what they are doing when there's no one around.

My own boarding kennel, which housed 175 animals, was nicely designed but far from perfect. The facility was expanded several times over a period of 15 years to meet increasing demands. The final addition, built a year before I took over, was a self-contained unit with 36 indoor/outdoor runs, plus kitchen, grooming room and reception area.

The main facility consisted of two- and three-tiered epoxy-coated steel cages of varying sizes. Boarders were exercised in relays in 25 outside runs. This involved lifting them in and out of cages and leading or carrying them to and from the building. Fortunately the majority soon learned the routine and went in and out on their own.

Monitoring Boarders

While having to handle that many dogs twice daily was a chore that required a staff of three, it provided the opportunity to monitor the dogs' physical condition every day. The dogs in the new unit were somewhat isolated and consequently less tractable.

Experienced, conscientious kennel aides are a great asset to any pet care facility. Members of our staff each worked in a specific section. Seeing familiar people reduced the time dogs required to adjust and feel at home. Having specific assignments gave the staff an opportunity to learn the dogs' idiosyncrasies so that changes in behavior could be spotted quickly. If a dog or cat didn't eat, developed a loose stool, seemed lethargic or showed any symptom needing further investigation, the person in charge of that animal reported to me, and it then became my responsibility to decide what action to take. Usually the animal would be checked to determine if examination by our veterinarian was required. If treatment was necessary, the cost of this service was added to the owner's bill. We collected all veterinary fees along with boarding and other charges when the dog was discharged.

If any doubt arose about a dog or cat's condition, the animal was immediately transferred to the isolation unit—a large, separate room not accessible from the main building, containing four large and six medium cages. Dogs confined there could be observed or treated day or night without disturbing the other boarders.

Working with the Plant

The new unit was comprised of a compact, red brick building with 4 ft. × 12 ft. runs on each side. The runs on the east side were covered, those on the west side were not; that may have had something to do with the sun field.

The concrete pad, like most I have seen, was not sufficiently graded. Don't believe what builders tell you, you need *double* the three-inch grading every ten to 12 feet that is normally allowed in most other types of construction projects. Both the inside and outside drains were too small to do the job and were continually getting blocked. Despite the fact that most solid matter was scooped up, we spent a small fortune on plumbers over the years. It was a major cause of irritation, frustration, inconvenience and unnecessary expense. Poor drainage remains a major flaw in much of today's kennel construction.

The inside of the indoor/outdoor unit was exactly 16 feet wide and slightly under 70 feet long. There was enough space for 36 four-foot square interior pens with a four-foot center aisle. The walls were covered with heavy-duty glazed tile from floor to ceiling. The ceiling was six feet high over the pens and eight feet high over the center aisle. Windows extended the length of the building along the center aisle, which precluded any chance of dogs escaping via that route.

Guttering extended the length of the building on either side of the center aisle, with three-inch drains every six feet; too small in diameter to do the job, they frequently became clogged with hair.

A section of the author's kennel showing the economical building design, which reduced construction, maintenance and operating costs to a minimum.

This view of the reception area and adjoining training paddock (right) illustrates the attractive, uncluttered design of the author's kennel.

The indoor/outdoor units as seen from above. Note the security fence in the foreground.

The author's facility as seen from the parking lot.

Pens were cleaned with a regular hose, using a power nozzle and an automatic detergent/disinfectant dispenser. This was a satisfactory method of sanitation, except during the summer when high humidity kept the pens from drying. The unit was not air conditioned, a serious oversight, although an automatically timed exhaust fan extracted stale air at regular intervals day and night.

The heating system consisted of hot water circulating through copper pipes buried in the concrete floor. The pens dried instantly in the winter and the dogs were never cold. Both inside and outside pens were squeegeed after hosing.

The dogs were customarily fed one meal a day, after their morning exercise. As a rule, new arrivals were not fed on their first day—which worked wonders for their appetite the remainder of their stay. Dogs not on special diets received the same basic dry food. They ate it willingly enough; in fact, most of them gained weight during their stay. Food was served in disposable dishes; any not eaten within 15 to 20 minutes was removed and dumped.

The original "L"-shaped building housing the older units was heated with hot water pipes and radiators in the winter and cooled by a giant central air conditioning system in the summer. The comfort factor was excellent, except during extraordinary weather cycles.

How Infection Can Happen

Ultraviolet lamps were used throughout the kennel to help minimize cross-infection. We experienced only one major problem: an uncontrollable outbreak of canine or "kennel" cough (tracheobronchitis) that happened one September when the kennel was filled to capacity.

How the incident occurred is worth telling, if only to illustrate the truth of the adage: *Nothing is foolproof; fools are too ingenious.* As a professional handler, I was on the road most weekends, often leaving Friday evening and returning Monday morning. As I was preparing to leave this one Friday evening, a customer arrived to collect his dog, leaving an empty pen in an otherwise full kennel. A new staff member was finishing up her chores. Five minutes before closing, I drove off and left her to lock up the kennel.

Returning to the kennel Monday morning after driving all night, I was greeted by the sound of a dog coughing that could be heard from two blocks away. In one of the pens I found a Pointer with a monumental case of canine cough. I vaguely remember demanding to know where it came from and being told it was a weekender that arrived just after I'd left on Friday.

Within a few days every dog in the place was coughing. Despite our efforts to contain the infection it spread throughout the kennel. I estimated that the incident cost me over $5,000 in lost income once word got around

The use of Italian tile and hanging plants brightens up the interior of Bob and Betty Beech's Beechline Kennels in Greensboro, N.C. The TV camera (upper left) allows the staff to monitor the boarders' activity without disturbing them.

While not essential, innovative designs, such as this custom brick bath stand, help make the interior of kennels and grooming shops look more attractive.

Chain link fencing has become a standardized feature of most commercial boarding kennels.

This badly fitting gate could trap dogs' feet, making it potentially dangerous; especially if no one was around.

24

that we had a kennel full of dogs dying of distemper. Two unhappy customers took their dogs to their own veterinarians, who incorrectly diagnosed the canine cough as distemper and started a panic.

Fortunately now that a vaccine is available, canine cough is not the problem it once was. Now there is parvovirus and coronavirus to worry about. As a result of this experience I established strict rules for admitting and discharging animals. The authority to take in boarders was restricted to senior staff members with enough know-how to screen incoming animals.

Experienced kennel managers develop their own formulas for success. I believe that whatever works for the individual is fine, but every phase of pet care has its built-in pitfalls that must be given ample consideration when rules are being established for running an operation.

2

One-Stop Pet Care

I HAVE MET many people and heard many ideas on a variety of subjects over the years. While living in Delaware I met a man who at the time was stationed at Delaware Air Force Base. During the normal course of conversation, he told me that prior to joining the military he had been in the dry cleaning business. As teenagers both he and his brother worked as part-time help in a veterinary hospital. From these unrelated sources of experience they planned to launch themselves into the automated kennel franchise business.

The Automation Concept

At first the brothers discussed the possibility of this futuristic project without serious intentions of implementing the idea. It was a sort of family joke, but eventually they decided to examine the prospects more seriously; rough plans were drafted, which in turn led to the building of a scale model.

During the early 1970s there was a rash of automated ideas presented that involved everything from the one I'm describing to rotating, self-cleaning astroturf dog runs, and self-cleaning pet stations. The reason they faded into oblivion may have more to do with acceptance at the time than whether the ideas were good or bad. Unfortunately, Americans were not yet ready for full-scale automation.

If you have been in a dry cleaners, you know roughly how the automated kennel system was going to work. Dogs were to be housed in fiberglass compartments that could be moved as required by a computerized conveyor belt, thereby eliminating the need for struggling with unruly dogs.

The administrative section of the building was comprised of a waiting and grooming room and merchandising area. The kennel consisted of 75 individual fiberglass compartments, a cleaning area for these compartments, storage for food and other supplies and 12 individual runs for exercising the dogs. The kennel compartments were transported as needed by a telescopic arm. The facility was temperature controlled and sanitized for maximum safety and comfort.

It was anticipated that boarders would be exercised twice daily. This would be controlled by computer. Twelve compartments would be moved into place at the end of the runs. The doors of the runs and the compartments would be opened simultaneously from the control room and closed once the dogs entered the runs. Each individual compartment would then be cleaned, followed by a closed-circuit TV safety check. After 30 minutes the dogs would be returned to their compartment to be returned to their stations.

The revolving astroturf runs were designed to receive an automatic steam cleaning after each group of 12 was exercised. To save time, the cleaning procedure was coordinated with the transfer of dogs to and from their stations.

At the time I questioned whether or not the dogs might feel too isolated because of the impersonal nature of the operation. I was told that since those in charge had no kennel chores to perform, part of their function would be to ensure that the boarders had adequate individual attention. A staff of three was considered necessary, but in an emergency the facility could be operated by one person.

As I recall, a prototype automated kennel was scheduled for construction somewhere in New Jersey. I never heard of it becoming operational. This idea was probably too ahead of its time—automation and computerization were considered a threat to mankind in the early 1970s. Perhaps in the future, if and when space and zoning preclude construction of conventional kennels, this idea will receive a second chance.

Although not ready for robotic automation, the pet industry has undergone some notable changes over the past few years. Kennel owners are finally taking a serious look at the total pet care concept; while it has yet to gain widespread popularity, the idea is starting to catch on.

Boarding Kennels and Veterinarians

In the past, the capacity for developing such a facility was limited to veterinarians. As most of them had far more work than they could cope with, they did not feel the need to be involved in the many problems associated with managing large-scale boarding and grooming operations. If anything was developed along that line it was not so much a complete pet-care facility as an animal hospital augmented with a few incidental sidelines. The doctor was the primary attraction.

Most individuals with a degree in veterinary medicine have not previously been inclined to work in a kennel where treating medical problems was not the primary function. In fact, it would be fair to say that the relationship between kennel management and veterinarians frequently lacked cordiality. This attitude, warranted or otherwise, made it impossible for laymen to recruit staff veterinarians. That situation may be changing. According to a study made for the American Veterinary Medical Association, the shortage of veterinarians that existed for the past ten or 15 years has been reduced, and it is projected that by 1990 there will be a surplus of 10,000 veterinarians in the United States. It is estimated that one result will be increased postprofessional education, leading to more specialization. Another will be a substantial increase in out-of-work DVMs looking for somewhere to practice.

Even if the number of available doctors does not exceed the increasing need of the general public, some veterinary school graduates are sure to reevaluate the benefits of working in conjunction with an established facility in preference to building a costly medical clinic and starting their own practice from scratch.

The cost of building, buying or leasing and equipping even a modest pet hospital constitutes a big burden financially. DVMs who can overcome their inherent reluctance to work for a businessperson instead of fellow medical professional have a lot to gain by stepping into a lucrative ready-made practice.

How does a kennel owner go about hiring a veterinarian to become part of the team? It is not easy. Anyone doing so must expect a lot of rejection. The enterprising manager of one total pet-care unit told me that he wrote to 700 DVMs licensed to practice in his state before finding one who was interested in what he was offering.

As long as the number of veterinarians working under traditional conditions remains sufficiently high there will be little change in attitude. Once we reach that inevitable saturation point it may be another story.

Looking still further into the future, it seems likely that preventive veterinary medicine will increase—with the emphasis switching to practicing preventive veterinary medicine rather than concentrating on curing already sick animals. Eventually this should reduce the number of animals requiring hospitalization, leaving more room for healthy animals. That would also reduce the income from hospitalizing sick ones, which means alternative income sources would need to be devised. The trend may force veterinarians and kennel operators to diversify their operations and eventually meet somewhere in the middle.

Total Pet-Care Contract

Another idea whose time may soon arrive is the total pet-care contract. A diluted version is being offered in some parts of the country, but so far most involve little more than glorified health insurance plans.

Total pet-care contracts would provide blanket coverage for all the animal's needs during a period of 12 months—from shots to grooming to boarding to surgery—for an all-inclusive annual fee, either on a total or limited scale, depending on cost of the premium. Obviously this could only be offered by a complete pet-care facility, which could be operated as a partnership, a company or by a cooperative team of independents renting space but operating as a unit.

3

Hobby Kennels

THOSE INVOLVED in breeding, showing or training dogs primarily as a recreational pastime may find it either convenient or necessary to incorporate their kennel facility and their home. This usually means converting the utility room, basement or garage.

Kennel as Part of Home

A friend of mine was recently quoted a price of $30,000 to remodel his garage and install half a dozen 4 ft. × 4 ft. inside pens and accompanying 4 ft. × 8 ft. outside runs. He decided to do the work himself with the help of a mason who did odd jobs on weekends, for only a fraction of the cost.

Another friend, whose work required his moving every few years, designed a sturdy portable unit made from concrete reinforcing rods and 2 in. × 1 in. galvanized wire fencing. It proved to be adaptable to almost every situation and allowed him to keep upwards of 20 Shelties without being unduly inconvenienced by these periodic transfers. I've seen the same unit installed in a garage, a barn, a basement and a utility room with only minimal modifications.

Designing Your Own System

To show what can be done with a little effort and only a moderate amount of cash, with the cooperation of Moses Animal Enclosures we converted makeshift dog pens into first-class, semipermanent kenneling.

This is a single or double isolation unit that attaches to an outbuilding and can be removed in minutes. The portable structure stands on a common red brick run, which can also be dismantled in a few hours. In many areas, this kind of unit is not prohibited by ordinances that forbid "permanent" kennels.

Note how far away the isolation unit is from the main kennels, seen in the right foreground, without spoiling the landscape.

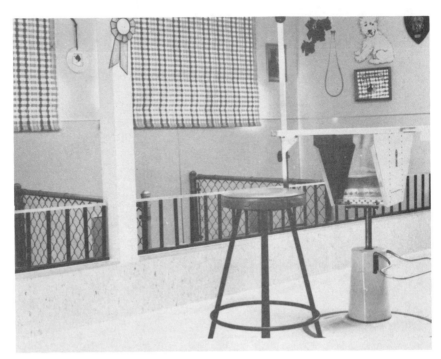

This facility, located in a residential area, is referred to by the owners as a "dog room" and as such successfully circumvents a local ordinance against neighborhood kennels. The "apartments," approximately four feet square by three feet deep (and about 12 inches below the level of the main floor), were constructed by enclosing and extending the rear patio. With the arcadia door in the living room open, the dogs do in fact live with the family.

The concrete floor slopes gently toward a single drain so the runs, normally covered with indoor/outdoor carpeting, can be hosed down whenever necessary.

The "dog room," which barely resembles a kennel, is fully equipped with its own kitchen and grooming area. Anyone inclined to do so could utilize this plan for any breed, regardless of size.

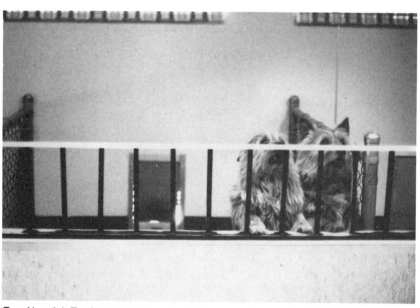

Two Norwich Terriers await the arrival of their evening meal with obvious enthusiasm.

A less elaborate "dog room" such as this can be installed in either a spare bedroom or utility room.

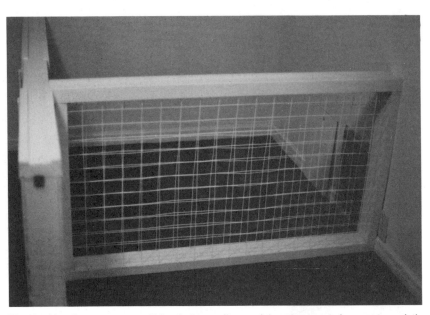

The double wire seems a good idea, but a smaller mesh is necessary to keep antagonistic kennelmates from rousting each other.

34

The most economical way to construct a hobby kennel is to convert an existing building. A snow fence, seen reflected on the kennel wall, was placed on top of these runs to provide partial shade and prevent the dogs from going over the top.

This kennel boasts an enormous exercise paddock where dogs can be turned out to run. Regular controlled exercise is essential to a dog's continued good health.

This old hen house was converted into an efficient hobby kennel at minimal cost.

The same system could be applied equally well to a garage or basement conversion as it was to the utility room we adapted.

How best to budget your money is the primary consideration. We opted for custom-built enclosures so that the available space could be utilized efficiently and it proved to be a cost-effective decision.

To house the required number of dogs, the utility room was widened an additional three feet. This involved moving an outside wall—a relatively easy task since it was frame and siding and not brick or block, which would have been more complicated. The job was accomplished in one weekend. All the materials were reused and the only cost was the price of approximately a yard of ready-mixed concrete and several sheets of plasterboard.

Moses Animal Enclosures of Medina, New York, custom manufacturer of kennel hardware, constructed the inside units to exact specifications. This proved to be both a blessing and a curse, because it allowed little or no margin for error as far as our measurements were concerned. Fortunately, we were almost precisely right—almost, but not quite. Our mistake was measuring the circumference of the room at approximately the four-foot level on the incorrect assumption that the walls were both square and plumb. They were neither. Luckily, the variation in the dimensions at floor level and the six-foot mark was not sufficient to create a major problem.

The lesson learned was not to take anything for granted. It is essential to measure both high and low points, and plumb the wall to insure that it is vertical. Be sure to note other possible irregularities, such as protruding water pipes, electrical conduits, etc., that cannot be moved to accommodate the rigid fence panels.

It is wise to check and double-check everything, especially if the room is not empty. Small miscalculations may make a substantial difference to the ease with which the enclosures can be installed once they arrive. Also, be certain you can get the panels into the room in one piece. This is not a problem as far as most garages are concerned, but utility rooms and basements are another story. You must have adequate clearance on both sides of the entry way to maneuver the panels around corners or down stairways. If in doubt make a mock-up of the panel using 2 in. × 1 in. furring strips. Don't *think* there is enough room—make sure.

The average 30-inch door will allow you to finesse panels up to seven feet through diagonally. The length will be determined by whatever solid obstructions you have on either side of the doorway that will restrict your movement. It is better to buy two four-foot panels rather than one eight-foot panel that you have to manhandle into position.

Make sure you specify the overall length of the panels coupled together. The average coupling adds about one-half inch to the length. Keep that fact in mind. The normal ceiling height is eight feet, but don't

An excellent twin unit standing on common red brick pad, this portable, freestanding two-dog run, manufactured by Moses Modular Animal Enclosures, can be erected or dismantled in less than ten minutes. Locating runs under large shade trees allows dogs to benefit from the early morning sun and still be protected from it during the heat of the day.

A portable pen is an inexpensive way to confine small dogs for short periods of time, and makes a great puppy pen when you need one in a hurry.

37

BEFORE: Aimhi Kennels' makeshift pens before the installation of Moses Custom Enclosures.

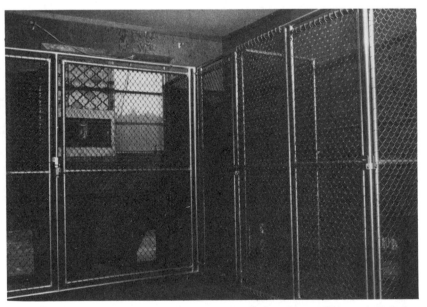

AFTER: The same utility area after custom manufactured kenneling was installed.

38

The room was widened an additional three feet to allow the installation of two more holding pens.

An overall perspective showing how the enclosures were tailored to the size and shape of the available space.

Aimhi Kennels' outside runs, surfaced with red brick, keep active terriers' feet in good shape. The dogs are also allowed to run in the large grass paddock in the foreground.

There are many ways to integrate runs with the landscape so that they are not an eyesore.

Runs surrounded by trees and shrubs tend to be less obtrusive.

Climbing vines and heavy foliage provide both shade and camouflage for these units.

bank on it. Unless security is a possible problem, standard six-feet-high panels are usually adequate for most people. Overhead covering can be added later for less than the cost of the taller panels.

A few breeds, such as Basenjis, are notorious fence climbers and will readily scale chain link enclosures. Apart from exceptions, four-feet-high fencing may prove sufficient for small- to medium-sized breeds.

Manufacturers of custom enclosures are anxious to help you. Consult them before you make your decision. They are in a position to advise and make useful suggestions. Take advantage of their expertise.

Depending on where you live, the cost of trucking fencing via common carrier or trucking line may be substantial. Be sure to shop around for the best deal. As all orders are shipped F.O.B. from the factory, you don't want to be in line for any unpleasant surprises because you haven't done your homework in that department.

When your new fencing arrives, check it carefully for damage and report any to the driver. Have him make a note of it on the invoice. Two of our latches were smashed and had to be replaced; so were two of the legs. The carrier is usually responsible for damage in transit, but you must submit a claim, often within a week or so, in order to receive compensation.

Additional Modifications

Backing up for a moment, if you anticipate painting or otherwise refinishing the walls inside the building, do it before installing the enclosures. It makes life a lot easier. There are a number of epoxy paints on the market that produce a lasting tile-like finish on both wood and concrete. Some require professional application for the best results. Never rely on dry wall alone. It will almost certainly get abused. I know of one case where a dozen German Shepherd Dogs did $18,000 worth of damage to the interior of a rented house. The renter, who owned the dogs, slipped off into the night without mentioning it to the landlord.

Whether you convert the garage, basement or utility room, you still need suitable outside exercise pens. They need not be of traditional construction or configuration. A lot depends on your esthetic viewpoint, the size of your breed and the amount of space you wish to allocate to the project.

Where restrictive local ordinances exist it is important to be in compliance. However, there are loopholes sometimes—if you can find them. One enterprising dog fancier who was denied a request to erect a kennel building on his property overcame the restriction against a "permanent kennel structure" by converting a mobile home to house his dogs.

Those who view traditional dog runs as unsightly or undesirable can use existing fencing or outside walls and make their exercise runs three or four feet wide around the perimeter of their property, disguising the inner

For coated breeds, plastic matting placed over pea gravel are a great combination. Note the self-watering device in the foreground. For easiest installation the matting should be installed before the fence is in place.

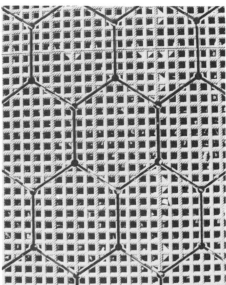

A closeup of the matting seen in the picture above.

Anyone who is reluctant to buy matting, which is expensive, will find common red brick the next best thing to use. This photo was taken ten minutes after the brick was hosed down. Concrete can take two or three times longer to dry under similar conditions.

fence by planting shrubs, vines and other suitable vegetation. This will effectively camouflage the runs and will not be an eyesore or spoil the landscaping. To some this is important, to others it is not. Much depends on one's priorities.

Run Surfaces

Run surfaces may be made from a variety of materials, including reinforced concrete, patio block, crushed cinder, pea gravel, sand, clay, dirt, shredded roofing shingles, crushed clam and oyster shells, common red brick or any other suitable substance. My preference is for common red brick. It is easy to install, equally easy to remove, washes down well and dries quickly. It also helps develop good, tight feet and blends favorably with any landscape. The cost of brick is comparable to concrete or less.

Concrete is probably the most popular and most expensive. Purchasing enough premixed concrete for two 10 ft. × 8 ft. runs costs around $60 to $80, plus a delivery charge if you happen to live beyond a specified distance from the concrete plant. All concrete should be trowel finished so that it is smooth and will not tear up the dogs' pads. A sealer also helps prevent the eventual powdering and surface erosion that tends to occur in time.

Screened pea gravel is supposedly good for the feet. However, some dogs are predisposed to dig under the gravel and bring up the dirt from underneath. This makes the runs muddy when it rains; for coated dogs that can be a problem. The solution is to bury four-inch concrete blocks in the ground before putting down the gravel. Digging then becomes impossible but the runs still drain well and can be hosed down as needed to keep the stones clean and reduce odor. Gravel is good for hobby kennels but I would not recommend it for commercial use.

Patio slabs on a bed of sand work reasonably well but are not as kind to the feet as bricks. Dirt is a problem when it rains. Packed crushed cinder is good and so is sand, but these surfaces are best used in exercise runs and not in heavily used enclosures.

Even if your dogs have the free run of the yard, as mine do, it is nice to have a place where they can be confined if necessary. Surfaced runs are also an asset during inclement weather and prevent a lot of mud and dirt from getting into the house. Owning a dog or two is not a valid reason for turning one's home into a kennel. Speaking for myself, I choose to have my dogs living in my home, not the reverse.

4

Care and Feeding Methods

KEEPING A KENNEL full of boarding animals in optimal condition is not easy. Many dogs and cats find boarding a stressful experience. Loosely defined, stress is anything that causes physiological and/or psychological strain, altering the physical, emotional or chemical elements in the body. Boarding, grooming, training, exercise, traveling, fighting, breeding, pregnancy, injury, disease, parasite infection, allergies and exposure to loud noise can all induce stress in varying degrees. To some animals, being deprived of daily affection would be very stressful.

Dealing with Stress

Like humans, animals react to stress in different ways. Some sulk or pine; others refuse to eat, or eat well and still lose weight. Some become destructive or aggressive, while others become hyper, wearing themselves out by fussing, barking and agitating on a nonstop basis. The latter also create additional stress for fellow boarders and kennel staff members.

Experienced kennel owners know it is important to keep avoidable stress to a minimum. That newcomers are the most effected is a pretty safe assumption. A good start in helping new arrivals adjust is to make them feel at home as quickly as possible. Their initiation should be as untraumatic as possible. It can make a great difference to the way they respond to their unaccustomed confinement, immediately and in the future.

Be sensitive enough to recognize and correct any problem situations that may exist at the time. Put first-timers next to calm, friendly dogs or cats that will show them a good example. Keep them as far away as possible from ill-tempered, aggressive or disruptive troublemakers.

The Well-Adjusted Boarder

Give boarders enough time to settle in without being bothered. Most dogs and cats adjust best if ignored until they start looking for attention. Emotionally well-adjusted pets move from the back of their runs to the front within a few days. First they become curious, and when they feel you present no threat, they soon invite friendly interaction. A wag of the tail as you pass, or a vocal greeting, may be the first indication to look for. From then on it becomes easy to establish and maintain a satisfactory rapport with the animal.

A few dogs and cats remain aloof and distant for the length of their stay. Providing they are tractable and present no problem, there is no need to spend an inordinate amount of time trying to win them over. I've known kennel people who treated this kind of rejection as a personal affront, and behaved as if this was a challenge to their integrity. There are bound to be animals that do not respond to you as well as others. Don't let that be a problem. However, if more pets dislike you than like you, you could well be in the wrong business.

Handle with Caution

Throughout this book I recommend handling all animals with caution. I once had a kennel aide who boasted that she had never even come close to being bitten. Then one day she arrived for work with 16 stitches in her leg. She was bitten by her own Dandie Dinmont while trying to stop a fight between two males. I shudder to think of the boy who was attacked by a St. Bernard while checking in with his mother who worked in a grooming shop. As the boy walked past the dog, which was going home after being groomed, it seized him by the head and ripped off the top of his scalp. The boy survived but was forced to undergo extensive reconstructive surgery. Why the dog attacked remains a mystery.

An acquaintance who owned a training kennel required more than 90 stitches to repair the damage inflicted by a German Shepherd he was training. He slipped and fell and the dog pounced on him. It can happen to anyone who is not paying attention. While caring for our charges in a kind and thoughtful way, we must keep in mind that one dog or cat in a thousand is potentially dangerous.

Exercise for Boarders

There are various ideas on how much exercise dogs and cats require while being boarded in order to remain healthy, and how big pens must be to be big enough. The size requirements for temporary pens may differ

These units, which are divided by a solid, four-foot-high concrete wall, permit what might otherwise be incompatible breeds to be housed adjacent to each other without problems. Given a choice, most small dogs would prefer to be isolated rather than intimidated. The inside units are similarly divided.

Although the low metal divider between these units prevents the males from urinating into adjoining runs, it cannot prevent aggressive dogs from intimidating more passive boarders.

46

Breed compatibility is something to keep in mind when constructing either a commercial or hobby kennel. Generally speaking, small breeds are most content with others of similar size and disposition. This is a small breed unit with runs 4 ft. × 8 ft.

The same facility as above also contains a special unit intended exclusively for giant breeds—something not seen very often. Note the extra-large popholes and 8 ft. × 16 ft. king-size runs that actually make the occupants seem small in proportion.

from permanent pet accommodation. However, tests have shown that dogs and cats derive no appreciable benefit from being housed in oversized pens when compared to so-called adequate accommodation for the size of the animal in question. Animals generally fail to derive any appreciable benefit from an overabundance of space and are equally contented with normal housing.

Because owners feel that in essence their pets are being incarcerated during their stay at the kennel, the question of how much freedom the dogs or cats receive becomes a major issue. Owners want their pets to have unlimited freedom, lots of exercise, and stay in oversized pens; they don't want them "locked up" all day. At home these same pets do nothing but eat and sleep all day long and never exercise.

While preparing this chapter I made a note of the amount of time my own dogs spent exercising themselves. The most energetic of the three is a Whippet; I calculated that left to her own devices she exercised less than one hour a day. Turned loose in the yard she is ready to lie in the sun or come back into the house in less than ten minutes. When exercised with an equally boisterous terrier, they both run out of gas sooner than that, especially during hot weather.

My personal view on exercising dogs boarding for two weeks or less is: the more restrained they are, the less opportunity they'll have to injure themselves. Many kennels allow dogs in indoor/outdoor units to have unlimited freedom to go in and out as they please. I see that as overly courageous, even irresponsible. Others may disagree; that's their prerogative. Some breeds and individuals are more energetic than others, but none should suffer unfavorable effects from being restricted to 30 to 40 minutes of exercise twice daily.

Dogs kenneled for weeks on end certainly need a good stretch in the paddock, depending on the breed. Even they usually take a few laps, sniff around some and then take a nap. A more practical approach is to use a treadmill to keep dogs toned if there is a need to do so.

Fed and exercised on a regular daily schedule, dogs soon adjust to their routine and learn to relieve themselves on cue, instead of more or less at random. The same thing happens to dogs when their owners are away at work all day.

When exercising dogs outside in warm weather during the heat of the day, kennel aides must be constantly on the alert for signs of heat prostration. This is especially important for breeds like Boxers, Bulldogs, Pugs and Pekes, which have inherent breathing difficulties. It can happen in a flash and prompt action must be initiated to save most victims.

Another asset of mass exercise is that it makes sanitation procedures easier. The runs remain clean between times, which helps reduce both odor and fly problems. Dogs that pop in and out at will are not as predictable in their habits. Some enjoy sliding through their excrement and getting covered in it.

I do not like to see dirty runs. My policy has always been: whoever sees it first, cleans up. Owners may expect their dogs to smell bad when they leave a kennel, but it makes a nicer impression if they leave cleaner than they arrived. Giving dogs complimentary baths after a week's stay or longer may be okay, but it is more profitable to talk the owners into paying for them.

With the excellent sanitation equipment available, ranging from power sprays to steam cleaners, coupled with the wide selection of chemicals to deodorize and sanitize, there is no reason to have a dirty kennel inside or out.

Which Diet Is Best?

Selecting your staple diet from the dozen or so best brands of dog food is a challenge. There are several considerations: palatability, nutritional density and easy digestibility. It is not so much a question of what food costs per bag as what it costs *per serving*. Yet the quality of the food is unimportant if dogs refuse to eat it.

A dry diet is the obvious choice. Tests indicate that dogs tend to prefer their dry food moistened with a little warm water. Picky eaters respond favorably to the addition of canned food (chopped beef, liver, chicken, etc.) to make a tasty gravy. To get poor eaters started, try dry cat food. Most dogs relish cat food!

When a diet is easily digestible, dogs unaccustomed to it are less inclined to develop gastric upset as a result of switching from their customary feed.

Certain diets produce better stools than others due to a stool-firming agent added to the formula. Well-formed stools facilitate cleaning operations, which can be important.

Whatever you choose, it should conform to the National Research Council's specifications of a complete and balanced diet. The Association of American Feed Control Officials (AAFCO) has ruled that a product cannot be labeled as complete and balanced unless it has undergone feeding tests with dogs and cats. Specific protocols have been established by the Pet Food Institute for proving claims relating to nutritional sufficiency for maintaining growth, lactation and so on.

A majority of dog and cat food companies maintain their own research facility and periodically publish reports on their findings. It would not be unfair to say that each company's research reports favor its own product.

In the final analysis, determining the value of one product over another is a highly subjective matter that each kennel owner must accomplish on his or her own.

For more information about foods and feeding, read *The Collins Guide to Dog Nutrition,* by Donald R. Collins, DVM; *The Evans Guide for Housetraining Your Dog,* by Job Michael Evans and *The Howell Book of Puppy Raising,* by Charlotte Schwartz (all published by Howell Book House).

Using individual gates leading from one run into another may be viewed as a minor inconvenience, but this adds over three feet to the length of each run that would be lost if th gates were placed conventionally.

5

Problem Dogs

WHEN WE THINK of "problem dogs" we usually conjure up visions of biting, screaming animals. That type of animal probably represents one in a thousand, but there are plenty of other problem types that also need consideration.

Personality Types

The *pugnacious, actively hostile dog* has usually learned to intimidate other members of its family. Consequently it expects to treat everyone else with similar contempt. Its confidence has systematically built up as a result of successful confrontations with humans until it has become a bully—regardless of actual size.

Confident of its ability to get away from assertive behavior, when aroused it walks around stiff-legged and bristling; hackles up (depending on the breed); tail up, probably flicking from side to side; ears up, or maybe laid back; challenging everyone with a hard, fixed stare. This type does not intimidate easily. It may growl or show its teeth and is inclined to attack without warning or provocation. There is no easy way to reach this dog or gain its respect. It expects to intimidate you, and in head-to-head confrontation would rather fight to the death than give an inch. Both dog and handler could be injured under such circumstances. Usually one of the larger breeds with a feisty temperament, this type is not too common. If confronted by one of these individuals, consider discretion as the better part of valor. Handle it as little as possible and with caution. Don't try to reform it, it's not worth the effort.

The *suicidal maniac* is a scared version of the pugnacious dog—with a dash of fear-biter or hysterical dog added for good measure. Unsure of itself, it may try both attack and escape tactics in turn with total disregard for its own safety. Too dumb to know when to quit, this type is potentially dangerous because anyone working with it stands a better than average chance of being bitten trying to save it from itself. This is one type that sometimes benefits from tranquilizers.

The suicidal type's posture is nervous and uncertain, tail down, ears back. It may tremble, whine or scream rather than growl. With experience it can be handled safely. The trouble is that this type can always find a way to self-destruct at the least provocation. Despite all its emotional problems, this kind of dog usually becomes attached to one member of the staff, who then has no problem with it.

The fear-biter's demeanor is characteristic of insecurity, suspicion dog. A paranoid, emotional cripple terrified for its own safety, it wants to be left alone. While not necessarily vicious, its aggressive behavior comes from overdeveloped instincts for self-preservation. This does not make its bite less painful, however. Cautious handling is advised.

The fear-biter's demeanor is characteristic of insecurity,, suspicion and distrust. It may stand with its head and tail down, back into a corner and growl, flinch or snap when touched or gnash its teeth if approached by strangers. It may also scream without being touched, refuse to be led and roll over onto its back, sometimes thrashing out with all four legs and/or urinating. Fear-biters are tense and sometimes react as the suicidal maniac: eyes darting around trying to see everything at once and looking for a means of escape.

This type of behavior should not be taken personally. The best way to handle a dog of this kind is to ignore its protests and act as if everything is fine. Given time, its defensive posture may lessen and it will settle in and be little or no trouble for the remainder of its visit.

Move and act deliberately and don't do sudden, unexpected things thay may startle a fear-biter and you'll probably win its confidence in time.

Emotional instability can stem from a variety of causes. Perhaps the most common is being kept isolated in the home and rarely going anywhere or seeing strangers.

The *hypertonic or hysterical dog* is a passive version of the fear-biter. Badly handled the hypertonic dog could turn into a fear-biter, but usually this type is too scared for that. In hypertonic cases the temperature and blood pressure becomes so elevated that the dog may collapse as if overcome by heat prostration. It may bleed from the nose, rupture the blood vessels around its eyes, have an epileptic-like seizure or go into shock.

This type of dog may be normal and friendly in its home environment and it would be difficult to convince its owner that you were not at fault if something unfortunate happened. Given time, the hypertonic dog responds to kindness and gentle handling.

The *grumpy old-timer* is often a good dog that has grown difficult with age. Sometimes they are neglected by owners just waiting for them to die. They are frequently overweight and infirm, suffering from arthritic and geriatric ailments. Old grumpies growl and try to sound tough. They sit or flop down rather than walk on a leash and maybe gum you a bit. If blind they insist on turning their back to you, hoping you'll go away. If deaf they are easily startled; let them know you're around by tapping on the floor.

They may have a heart condition or other health problems so care should be taken to see that they don't get excited. Their behavior is more in the nature of a protest than active aggression. Like some old folks we know, they need patience and understanding.

The *hyper types* can't stand still for one moment; they are too friendly, with too much energy. They drive you nuts.

The *schizophrenic* is a Jekyll and Hyde: good one moment, bad the next. It may start off friendly and suddenly turn without warning. This dog has learned through experience that when it snaps at people they leave it alone. If you fail to react as expected the dog will often resume a passive posture. Be firm without starting a fight.

In addition to those mentioned above, there are also combination types that can present a real challenge.

Your attitude plays a significant part in the way dogs behave. Usually a firm, business-like attitude beats both too much affection and too much brutality. If you anticipate having problems, you will. On the other hand, if you feel confident about handling a dog it will be better behaved. That's not to suggest that dogs will always be perfect. Even good dogs become difficult at times. As soon as you concede that a dog is unmanageable, it will be. Handled with reassuring confidence most dogs learn to trust those who take care of them.

There is a simple but effective slip lead on the market for use in handling uncooperative dogs. It enables the handler to release the animal without putting his hands on the dog. A catchpole for dangerous dogs can be made with a length of 3/4 inch electrical tubing and some strong rope. I never like having these gadgets around because using them becomes a habit, whether they are really needed or not.

Most troublesome dogs settle down in a day or two if treated correctly. The apparent need for human approval seems to override most other considerations.

Handling Unfriendly Dogs

Those unfamiliar with techniques for handling unfriendly dogs soon learn that the koochy-koochy-koo approach can be a quick ticket to the hospital emergency room. Friendly or not, most dogs can be controlled with comparative safety, when done correctly. The golden rule is to stay away from the end that bites. Most pet-care professionals bitten by their charges admit to having been at least partly responsible because of their own carelessness when handling the animal.

Fortunately, most pets are reasonably well mannered and amenable to being handled by strangers. Experienced professionals should know enough to be most wary of dogs whose owners insist, "He wouldn't bite a fly." Owners have no way of knowing what course an animal's behavior will take, except from experience. The "He won't bite" syndrome comes from wishful thinking and the owner is frequently wrong.

Dogs bite because they are dogs. Making a distinction between good dogs and bad dogs is a waste of time. Stay around dogs for long enough and eventually one will get you. Dogs bite for any number of reasons. Fear is probably the main cause. Dogs rarely behave aggressively toward people well outside their own territory. Most bite cases occur in or around the dog's home. One study of bite statistics showed that 90 percent of the bite wounds reported were from dogs owned by a neighbor, relative, friend or the victim's family.

As owners may serve as territorial reference points, some dogs may see an attempt to separate them from their owners as an act of aggression. This makes the initial contact with dogs the most hazardous. There are numerous indications that a dog objects to being handled. Growling can be both offensive and defensive in nature. Either way it usually means *don't push your luck*. Most insecure dogs would rather run than fight; not having a choice, they may choose to use their teeth. There are no easy solutions to the problem until the dog is separated from its owner.

Sometimes a dog will bite or snap without warning. That is only partly true, of course. You get plenty of indirect signs: a subtle stiffening of the body, a slow turning of the head, a bristling of the hackles, a twitch of the tail, a hard stare; any one of which should be warning enough for an experienced professional.

Eye expression often provides the best clue to what is on a dog's mind. Usually, a dog with an honest eye rates as trustworthy. One with a troubled or wild eye merits caution. I once heard an honest eye in a dog described as having an expression similar to Billy Graham's. Sounds feasible to me.

Once separated from their owners most dogs become more tractable. Reaching for small dogs held in their owner's arms is risky business. The easiest solution is ask the owner to put the dog down onto the countertop so you can reach for it while it is momentarily disoriented. Scoop it up under your arm before it knows what's happening.

If you have to take a dog from its owner's arms, reduce the risk of being bitten by first taking hold of its leash; keep the leash taut while reaching your other hand under its belly.

54

Picking a small dog up off the ground also involves an element of risk. Grasp the leash about 12 inches from the collar, and using a quick scooping motion, reach under its stomach at the point of balance, pick it up and tuck it under your arm. Again, keep the leash tight so it cannot turn its head and grab you. Sometimes one will thrash around some, but if you hold on tight it will soon calm down.

A tricky situation can develop if a nervous dog settles back into a corner and defies you to extricate it from its pen. Put your hand in and you'll be sorry. If you cannot coax it to the front of the pen, reach in with a loop or leash and secure it around the dog's neck. Once the dog is caught pull it gently toward you and scoop it up as already described. Sometimes it helps if you leave a short length of line attached to the dog's collar for a day or so. Once dogs learn they are not going to be harmed, most of them become friendly and easy to handle.

Some of the problems groomers and kennel owners have to deal with are associated with negative preconditioning that occurs when young puppies make their first visit to the veterinarian's office for a shot. That can sometimes turn into a traumatic experience. It does not reflect on the veterinary profession in any way, but try explaining to a puppy that the insertion of a rectal thermometer followed by the injection of cold vaccine is not taking liberties. Such an experience can and does produce a fear response. Most humans feel the same way about visiting their dentist. All other considerations aside, I doubt if any veterinarian ever stopped to contemplate the fact that he or she may be responsible for the way a puppy interacts with other pet-care professionals for the rest of its life.

A first-time boarder or grooming client deposited alone in a cage in strange surroundings can soon become intimidated by unfamiliar sights and sounds, especially the barking and screaming of other dogs. Imagine yourself in its place. How would you feel?

Hearing other dogs in what sounds like distress can induce fear in a puppy or young adult that has no idea of what is in store for it. If by some misfortune you happen to have a screamer in that day a newcomer might develop contagious hysteria from hearing what might be an otherwise well-mannered dog making so much noise.

A bad experience or two will create an avoidance response in an emotionally undeveloped individual. That could mean becoming paranoid over anything associated with boarding, grooming or veterinary care.

Owners will tell you that their dogs knew where they were going because they shivered from the moment they entered the car. Let's face it, most dogs ride in the car only when going to the grooming shop, kennel or veterinary hospital. It doesn't take a canine Einstein to figure out that it's going to one undesirable place or another.

We all are the product of our experiences, they say. I expect that also applies to dogs. Those with bad past experiences may never learn to trust strangers. Good pet-care professionals try to overcome distrust with kindness and understanding, without getting their ego involved.

Accept dogs for what they are, and that some will like you and others won't. If you do your job, the percentages will be in your favor. Not all dogs will be amiably disposed to everyone. It's no big deal, even if it does make you feel good when the owner expresses surprise that the dog likes visiting the kennel. I knew a groomer who would put hostile males into a pen where he'd previously kept bitches in heat. Most of them couldn't wait to return to the shop.

A Sobering Case History

Occasionally you encounter a really dangerous dog. Fritz was one of those. I was visiting with my veterinarian when an older couple brought Fritz in for his booster shots. Doc asked me to help him lift the dog onto the examining table. I should have declined when I saw that the dog was wearing one of those disgusting German-made pinch collars. It has always been my contention that if you need that kind of a collar to control it, you've got the wrong dog for you.

As I grasped the dog by the scruff of the neck I inadvertently trapped my index finger between the prongs. When the dog started struggling I almost lost my finger. Worse than that, I was unable to release the dog after the shot was given. The owners were concerned only about their poor baby, as they called him. I finally untangled myself; Fritz just missed me as I turned him loose.

Although not the biggest German Shepherd Dog in the world, Fritz was big enough; he thought he was king of the hill and I didn't intend to argue with him about that. About six months passed before I saw Fritz again. He was bigger, stronger and meaner; his owners had less control over him than when I first saw him. They wanted me to board the dog for two weeks. I didn't know it at the time but he'd been banned from the other two kennels in town.

Trying to sidestep any trouble I got the owner to put him directly into one of the indoor/outdoor units. That was a smart move; not so smart was failing to check that the pen had been latched securely.

An hour later I opened the door into the main unit and found Fritz waiting there, every hair on his body standing upright. I stood motionless, holding the door open while the dog strutted past me and into the main reception room. Having read Konrad Lorenz's book *On Aggression* I knew this dog was going to be a problem. Even if I'd never read a book in my life I would have known that. Stiff-legged, head up, tail flicking from side to side, ears forward, eyes wide open, his whole attitude was challenging. It was lunch time and I was alone in the kennel. Grabbing a grass broom I followed the dog. I was terrified that an unsuspecting customer might walk in off the street and be attacked.

I carefully circled around Fritz and managed to lock the front door. I was still worried that the dog might decide to exit through the ¼-inch plate glass. While the dog was sniffing around the store I opened the door leading to the outside runs and opened the first gate so he would be trapped if he went outside. My intention was to steer him outside and into the open run. No good. He declined to cooperate.

Up to this point I'd avoided looking the dog in the eye to avoid provoking an attack. He never made a move toward me until we made eye-to-eye contact. He circled slightly and charged. He was not bluffing, but neither was I. As he charged I jabbed the stiff broom at his chest, stopping him in his tracks. Traction on the polished tile floor was not good. Regaining his balance he attacked again, slashing at the harsh bristles with his teeth. All he got for his trouble was a mouth full of grass.

We jousted back and forth for five or ten minutes as I tried to force him outside. His attitude had changed. His ears were back, his tail down and he was messing all over my nice, clean floor. Finally he retreated into the washroom, a long, narrow room with a shower stall at the far end, where Fritz entrenched himself. I locked him in there, a little after the fact, unfortunately.

No serious harm had been done to either of us and I wanted to keep it that way. Putting on the padded sleeve we used for training guard dogs, I broke the broom handle short enough to use in one hand and went in after Fritz. Taken by surprise and completely intimidated he bolted outside and into the run I'd opened for him. He could have done that at the start and saved us both a lot of energy.

Although he never quit growling at me, the rest of Fritz's stay was otherwise uneventful. When the owners came for him I told them to never bring him back. I didn't go into details, but it took me over two hours to clean the feces from the floor and walls of three rooms. I could live without that. Besides, he ruined a new broom and I never liked destructive dogs.

If there's a point to this story, and I believe there is, I suppose it illustrates that when you do dumb things you have to suffer the consequences. I certainly did.

6

Handling Large Breeds

"**O**H, MY ACHING BACK!" How often we hear that lament. Unfortunately, back strain is one of the hazards of the dog business. Dogs seem to have a knack in making a hurt to your person, whether by wriggling while you are carrying them in your arms or, if on a leash, by pulling you off balance when you are not paying attention.

Pain in the neck, shoulder and lower back area is the most common reason why people visit their doctor. According to medical reports, the chief cause of these problems is bad posture and unnecessary strain caused by improper lifting techniques or similar muscle abuses.

Muscle strain or bad posture can also be responsible for the neck and shoulder pains. As one doctor described it, much that applies to the lower back in the way of torn ligaments and overtaxed muscles can also apply to the rest of the body.

Do not bend from the waist to pick up large dogs. Bend at the knees when lifting any heavy object, instead of stooping over. Keep the back straight and let your legs do most of the work. Keep your body square to the front. Never reach to one side or the other; doing so creates an uneven pull on the back muscles that could cause serious injury.

Get someone to help you lift big dogs onto the table or into the bathtub. Do not overestimate your own strength. If forced to handle big dogs while working alone, use steps, ramps or other devices.

Finally, do regular back-strengthening exercises to minimize the risk of injury and back strain. In most parts of the country the YMCA conducts special exercise classes to help people keep their backs strong and supple.

If you do sustain an injury, most medical experts advise getting as much rest as possible to encourage rapid recovery. You cannot work off a back injury. Trying to do so might result in a chronic condition that could plague you for life. In most cases seeing a doctor is advisable, just in case.

This outside run utilizes all the available yard space by extending from the enclosed patio to the exterior wall.

7

There's More Than One Way to Board a Cat

CAT BOARDING can be a blessing and a curse. While the majority of cats are as easy to handle as most dogs, their incredible speed and agility make them a much greater security risk. In addition, a really bad cat can create far more problems than it's worth in terms of boarding fees.

Housing Systems

The majority of kennels that also board cats usually adopt one of three basic housing methods: centralized, communal or scattered.

The *centralized* cattery concept seems to be the most popular. A section of the facility is allocated exclusively to cats, keeping them totally segregated from the dogs. Cat owners and cat lovers in general appear to believe that this is the most suitable arrangement, but in fact the system has questionable merit because it keeps the cats in close proximity to each other, courting trouble in the event of a sudden outbreak of some highly contagious feline disease.

Communal confinement, where cats are housed together in a large building or one big room equipped with a variety of hideaways, bedding and furniture to create a living-room atmosphere, is probably the most arbitrary and least desirable method from all practical standpoints. However, a surprisingly large number of cat fanciers like the idea of having their pet free, meaning not locked in a cage, with a lot of nice friends to play

60

with in this home-like setting. For obvious reasons, this type of facility accepts only spayed or neutered animals. Otherwise there would be hair flying in all directions.

Perhaps the biggest drawback of communal confinement is that some cats vanish immediately upon introduction into the colony and are not seen again until it is time to send them home. Sometimes the owners have to go into the building and retrieve the shy or timid ones who are reluctant to show themselves to strangers, which also makes it difficult if not impossible to monitor their condition effectively.

Litter, drinking water and food, usually dry or semi-moist, are placed in strategic locations to be available to all. While the system seems to work for some, it does raise serious questions concerning the infinite potential for assorted disasters that could occur within the limits of statistical probability. I prefer to have more control over the situation.

The main concern kennel owners and managers should have is how to best care for animals entrusted to their safekeeping in a conscientious and responsible way, so they can be returned to their owners safe, sound and healthy. There are all kinds of frills that, while making a boarding facility outwardly more appealing and attractive, add nothing to the functional and practical aspects of good animal husbandry. For just that reason there is a strong case to be made for the *scattered* method of boarding cats— having cat pens randomly situated throughout the kennel, separated from each other by dog pens. This method minimizes the possibility of cross-infection if a serious disease is inadvertently introduced by an infectious carrier showing no obvious clinical symptoms of sickness at the time of admission.

Contrary to what some cat lovers may believe, cats adapt quite readily to being surrounded by dogs. In fact, they may adjust to the situation better than the dogs—especially terriers. Incidentally, as terriers hate having either dogs or cats housed above them, terriers should be kept in an upper tier whenever possible. This will keep them from fretting or being unnecessarily disruptive and noisy. Obviously, where dogs are housed in indoor/outdoor runs this problem does not occur.

In addition to the more popular housing methods already described, some of the newer establishments have family units or suites where dogs and cats belonging to a family are kept together. While it seems like a good idea, some of these animals are not overly fond of each other and it pays to keep a sharp eye on them when they first arrive to make sure they get along as amicably confined in close quarters as they do at home.

Feeding and Sanitation

Cats need food, water and litter. They like to have an elevated bed and somewhere to hide, if they feel so inclined. They must be kept comfortably warm and away from cold drafts.

An increasing number of kennels now offer indoor/outdoor cat units.

Kitty condos are becoming a fashionable addition
to many kennels. These units are four feet wide,
two feet deep and three feet high.

As a rule, the cheapest clay litter you can buy is adequate. There are an assortment of utensils that can be used to hold the litter, but the most practical and economical are the cardboard boxes that hold canned dog or cat food, cut in half height-wise. Line the bottom with newspaper and use little more than an inch or so of clay. You can see at a glance if the cat is passing normal stools and is urinating sufficiently. Every few days, or as soon as the box gets smelly, it can go in the trash and be replaced with a new one. This also eliminates the need to deodorize and sanitize litter pans.

Keep in mind that cats are abnormally sensitive to a wide variety of chemical products, and should not come into contact with most cleaners customarily used for dogs. This is especially important with products containing phenol derivatives or by-products, which are found in most disinfectants. Read the labels carefully, and if you are not sure, ask someone who is. Your local veterinarian should be willing to help you identify potentially hazardous products.

Feeding can be a problem, and owners are usually little or no help in that department. They usually bring in an assortment of special concoctions, none of which the cats will eat. Others have secret tips for you ("He loves anything that is topped with puff rice" or "She can't resist bacon bits").

As a rule, finding the right food is a question of trial and error. When you find the magic formula, write it on the cat's file card so you'll know next time. Don't trust your memory; after awhile everything becomes a blur.

Disposable paper food dishes save time and effort by eliminating the need to wash and sanitize dirty pans. If the cat does not eat the food, dump it. Cats rarely eat stale food.

Being nocturnal by nature, problem eaters sometimes benefit by being fed at night around closing time. That is best determined by trial and error.

Health Questions

Cystitis (an ailment associated with the urinary tract) is a common problem in felines. Reportedly, high ash content in the food plays a significant role in the development of the disease and resulting bladder stones. If the cat does not seem to be urinating normally or has difficulty when doing so, the matter should be referred to a veterinarian who can prescribe medication to help reduce discomfort and remedy the ailment.

If a cat is on a prescription diet, it must stay on that diet, but the owner should be willing to provide sufficient food for the duration of its stay.

Having to give cats medication can be a problem. Liquids are not too bad but pills can be a hassle. Instead of sticking your finger down a cat's throat and being bitten for your trouble, use the eraser end of a regular wooden pencil to ease pills into the back of the gullet. You have to develop good reflexes and be willing to stick to your guns. Cats can be very stubborn about having something they don't want to swallow forced down their throat. You must be as determined as they are.

63

Finally, make sure that cats accepted for boarding have had all their shots. Some kennels and catteries require a vaccination certificate as proof that shots are current. This is a good policy to adopt.

Above all, never admit a cat or kitten with runny eyes and nose, that is sneezing or wheezing or looks "under the weather." Feline ailments are often fatal to susceptible individuals. It's better to be wrong but safe than risk introducing a highly infectious disease into your facility. Because cats are often transported in carriers, ask the owners to take them out so you can examine the animal before the customer leaves.

Handling

Most cats are friendly enough after a few days. As a breed, Siamese are probably the least cooperative. Unneutered toms are the most aggressive and smelliest. For handling the occasional troublemaker, wear protective gloves. Cat scratches and bites are painful and also prone to infection. There is no merit in allowing yourself to be injured by an ill-tempered animal. Take whatever precautions are necessary to insure personal safety.

Odor Control

For neutralizing cat odor we suggest Dualle products. This company has been involved in odor control for many years. The following methods are being used in many catteries nationwide. Dualle products are also used to deodorize the majority of cat shows around the country. Used as directed, the products mentioned are nontoxic to both animals and humans. It should be noted that odor control is not a substitute for sanitization. However, no amount of soap and water alone will destroy all cat odors. The Dualle odor control program does, and has received the Pet Pride Seal of Approval.

For eliminating airborne odors use *Formula Air Freshener*. This product does not numb the sense of smell like some other products. It eliminates odors by the process of oxidization. There are many ways to get this product into the air. For areas with good air circulation a wick bottle or drip sanivator should work adequately. In areas with poor air circulation a fan can be used or the air freshener can be added to the humidifier, forced air heating system or central air conditioning system to control the entire area serviced by the unit.

To eliminate odors at the source use *Odor Control Concentrate*. This is a residual deodorant that destroys odors on contact. It can be diluted at a ratio of 5 ounces to one gallon of water.

If litter odor is a problem, thoroughly clean the litter pans and spray the bottom of the pan with a coarse wetting spray. Add litter to the pan and spray the litter, mixing it up after spraying in order to obtain a uniform distribution. Remove solids daily, respraying the litter each time. This will also eliminate urine odor.

Similar application can be made on any color-fast material, including carpets, drapes and upholstery. Before using on expensive materials, check to be certain that they are color-fast.

For urine, fecal matter and male cat spray use 2 ounces in a pint of water. To knock down odors, first spray and then remove solids. Use a coarse, saturated spray on the area. For heavy contamination a second application may be needed. Remember that some cats have a stronger odor than others.

For shampooing or steam cleaning, add 6 ounces of Odor Control per gallon of shampoo or cleaning solution. This may reactivate the odor, causing more airborne odor; treat that as indicated earlier.

Odors should disappear in a day or two and not return unless there is recontamination. Odor control has always been a problem associated with cat boarding. Now there is a remedy that works.

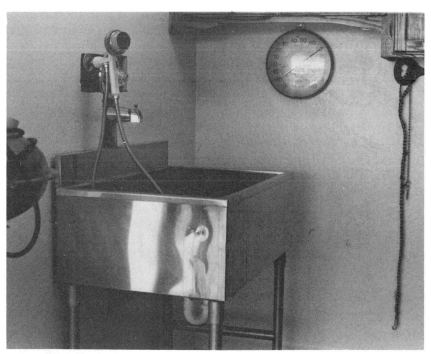

A small bathtub is easily installed either in the utility room or the garage.

8

Peak Boarding Management

MAINTAINING AN ACCURATE tally of all boarding reservations is the basic requirement for efficient management of peak boarding periods. With proper planning you can avoid the hassle of having more dogs and cats arrive than you are equipped to accommodate, and you will also know in advance whether or not you need extra help. By monitoring reservations you will be able to determine if it is necessary to restrict the number of new customers you can accept in order to ensure there will be room left for the regulars who sometimes fail to make reservations until the last minute. Having to reject regular patrons because they forgot to call is not good policy.

The trick is devising a system that everyone can understand and use, yet is not time consuming. The one outlined here has been well tested and is easily adapted to suit most operations.

Reservation System

THE RESERVATION SLIP. A reservation slip, which can be your regular file card, is pulled when the customer calls. New customers are given temporary slips with all the essential details noted: the owner's name, address and phone number, the breed, size and sex of the dog. The information on the animal is important if you have different types of accommodation—big pens, small pens, indoor/outdoor runs, etc. The information from the reservation slip is later entered in your desktop diary.

KEY NIGHTS. The first step in identifying peak periods is to identify "key nights." For example, during the Christmas holidays December 24 would be considered the key night. After all the scheduled boarders arrive on Christmas Eve the number of kennel occupants will remain the same until after the 25th, when boarders start going home. New Year's Eve would also be a key night. For Thanksgiving, which is always a Thursday, the preceding Wednesday would be the key night. During the summer, Friday and Saturday are usually the busiest.

RESERVATION CHART. Having identified your key nights, make a reservation chart (sample follows). Divide a sheet of ruled paper into four vertical columns. Write "Key Day & Date" at the head of each column. Allow one vertical line for every five or ten pens, indicating your maximum capacity. You can use separate columns for cats, large or small dogs, doubles or any other designation that suits your needs.

Make a check ($\sqrt{}$) mark for each reservation for the night(s) indicated. Allow space at the bottom of each column to record cancellations in the same way.

Update the reservations chart from the reservations slips, when convenient to do so. It pays to mark each slip as it is entered to avoid duplication. From the chart you can see at a glance what space remains available.

With accurate record keeping, you will know what to expect. Over a period of time it will become possible to estimate the average cancellation rate for your business, thereby allowing you to overbook knowing that the final count will be near capacity. Such knowledge can also provide a basis for limiting the number of weekenders accepted during seasonal peaks. Admitting animals that arrive on Friday and go home on Monday, leaving pens empty the remainder of the week, shows a poor return.

When a full house is anticipated part-time help may be needed. Knowing what to expect enables the kennel operator to make appropriate arrangements and not be caught napping.

SAMPLE RESERVATION CHART

	KEY DAY & DATE	KEY DAY & DATE	KEY DAY & DATE	KEY DAY & DATE
5				
10				
15				
20				

PERMANENT CALENDAR. In addition to keeping tabs on the reservations and cancellations, another permanent record in the form of a calendar is needed to record other pertinent information that might be important in helping analyze your figures at a later date.

Every night, record the actual head count in the kennel at the time. Add any other information that may be important: holidays, weather conditions, anything that might contribute to the kind of business you are doing—good or bad.

Over the years these records will help you pinpoint changing trends and perhaps provide the information you need to establish profit margins, contemplate expansion, secure a loan or sell the business.

For kennels using a computer—the management tool of the future—all information can be stored on a disk and made available for instant reference whenever needed.

9

The Formula for Success

WHY IS IT that two individuals with apparently equal ability can go into the same type of business, in the same town, in comparable locations and one becomes a big success while the other fails? Even if, as some might contend, there wasn't enough business to go around, each should theoretically have garnered about an equal share of the available market.

While being unconventional may under certain circumstances indicate character, most shoppers, including those shopping for kennels and grooming parlors, respond most favorably to the conventional approach to customer relations. Being a confirmed individualist rarely pays off as well as being traditional—in a business sense.

You can increase your potential for success as a kennel or grooming parlor owner by sticking to a reliable, established formula for obtaining the best results when dealing with the general public.

1. **Cater to the Customer.** Your number-one ambition should be to please your customers. They keep you in business. Learn their individual likes and dislikes. Make them feel that you are always interested in them and their pets. Don't be afraid to give them that little extra service. They will appreciate it and tell others how wonderful you are. Word-of-mouth advertising is both the cheapest and the most effective. Always thank customers for their patronage. It makes them feel important. Be an ego builder and not an ego crusher.

2. **Build an Image.** All businesses need steady, solid promotion 365 days a year. Part of building an image is self-promotion, using ads, handbills, signs and even radio advertising when you can afford it. There's an old horse-trading adage that says, "Praise all the faults and let the virtues speak for themselves." That means avoid negative attitudes. People tend to pick up on them immediately. Even favorable impressions can suffer unless you use some charm and personality to "sell" yourself as well as your services.

Answering the telephone should not fall to whomever happens to be nearest when it rings. Over the years we have had occasion to call numerous pet-care facilities from time to time. In a high percentage of instances the person who answered our call was harassed, impatient or uninformative to the point of being rude. Potential customers call seeking both information and reassurance. Give it to them.

If and when they visit your place of business, they should find a clean, well-organized, well-lighted reception area that is relatively free from doggie smells and odor. That helps to reinforce the favorable impression you created to attract the customer to your kennel in the first place.

3. **Work as a Team.** Your employees must conform to your image. The satisfaction customers get while patronizing your kennel is often in the employees' hands. Staff members should work as a team, not as a bunch of disinterested individuals. Teach them what you want them to do and how and when to do it. Accept no compromise. It's your reputation on the line. Praise employees in public. Correct them in private.

Don't endanger their loyalty with a "do as I say and not as I do" philosophy that fosters resentment.

4. **Plan Ahead.** Teamwork lightens the load. Good planning can leave you with more time for management work and customer relations. Keep a realistic schedule that you and your staff can handle. Train an assistant. Put him or her in charge and take the day off periodically. It will do you good and help your assistant gain confidence and experience in case of an emergency.

5. **Look for Profit.** Your purpose for being in business, unless you are some kind of nut, is to earn a living. That means you must show a profit. Profit depends on what is left after you pay all your bills. Many of those who work cheap may be deluding themselves about the amount of profit they are making.

If you want a reasonable profit margin you must keep expenses in line. Make a list of both fixed and variable expenses. Rent is an example of a fixed expense. You have to pay it whether you do any business or not. Shampoo is an example of an expense that varies according to the amount of work you do and is classified as variable. Determine your break-even point—the point at which your income and expenses are equal. Use that to determine what changes are needed for your business investment to show a satisfactory return in proportion to the amount of money, time and effort you are investing.

6. **Pay Your Civic Dues.** Your opportunity for expansion could be related to the growth of the community in which your business is located. You pay your civic dues by actively supporting efforts to improve your community through participation in civic-minded organizations. Doing your share also helps enhance your image. *Caution:* Take only what you can handle. It is better to be involved in a few projects that accomplish something than a whole bunch going nowhere.

If this formula sounds like plain, common sense, that's because it is. Then why isn't everybody doing it?

10

Who's the Boss?

NOT SO LONG AGO every journeyman dreamed of being his own boss. There were times when being self-employed was a source of pride and personal satisfaction. Today the trend seems to favor working for big companies that offer ample fringe benefits. However, there are still an estimated 10 million small businesses in this country, each employing an average of four people. For many it is an uphill struggle; often the biggest stumbling block is the United States government. Instead of helping the small businesses in their fight for economic independence, Uncle Sam seems to delight in penalizing them. Why do they do it, then? The most naive answer I've ever heard is, "So I can be the boss and become independent."

The Client Calls the Shots

If you are self-employed you still have a boss—the customer or client. Unless you can keep your boss the customer happy, you have little hope of staying in business, and your new boss can be hard to please.

As a boss the customer may be unaware that his or her demands are unreasonable, impossible and possibly ridiculous. (If ignorance of one fact or another were a crime, sooner or later we'd all end up in jail.) So, the boss must be handled with tolerance and understanding. After all, the boss is always right. Unless you are independently wealthy, you cannot afford to offend, upset or irk the boss. He or she may be unreasonable, demanding, ungrateful, arrogant, petulant and a pain in the butt, but don't let on that you noticed.

Be friendly, helpful, understanding and patient. Your livelihood depends on it. You cannot afford the luxury of offending anyone that helps you pay the rent. Maintain your poise. Remember that sometimes the way you smile is more important than the way you do your job.

There is a psychological reason why many owners who bring in neglected dogs make such impractical demands. It's called guilt. They know that their dog is in bad shape and that they are at fault. This realization puts them on the defensive. If they make absurd excuses in an effort to explain away their dog's condition, accept the explanation. In a way it is a form of apology. If you unwittingly injure their self-esteem it will only make them resentful, which in turn could manifest itself in outright hostility. Such was the case when the owner of a badly neglected Old English Sheepdog found his dog not groomed to his satisfaction. When first told that his dog was too neglected to comb out and would have to be clipped down he seemed resigned to the idea. Admitting that he never brushed or combed the dog, he asked the groomer to do what she thought was best. Yet, when he collected the dog and found it had been clipped to the bone he became incensed.

"What kind of job do you call that?" he screamed. "You've ruined my dog!" He then consoled the dog by saying things like: "Oh, you poor dog. Look what they've done to you. They've made you feel embarrassed." Slapping his money on the counter, his parting shot was, "I'll know not to bring my dog back here again."

It's not uncommon for guilt to be expressed as hostility. When this individual said the dog was embarrassed, he meant that he (the owner) was embarrassed. After all, he would have to justify the dog's sorry appearance to his friends and family. The easiest way to do that was to shift the blame to the groomer. If the dog could have been combed out, even at an astronomical cost, he would have been much happier. Seeing the dog shaved down reinforced the fact that he was to blame for the dog's condition.

Some dog owners are less sensitive than others. In fact, some are totally oblivious. Some are not fazed whether you clip their dog down or not. The trick is to distinguish one type from the other.

Keep in mind that people come into your shop or kennel to spend money. Anyone with cash to spend has a variety of options. Years ago people were obliged to patronize the business nearest to home, but today no one thinks twice about loading their pet into the family car and driving to a competitor willing to cater to their wants.

Why They Need You

In addition to having their dog boarded, customers come to you for very basic reasons.

1. **Their dog needs to be groomed.** The urgent need to have a dog groomed might be brought about by the sudden realization that the animal has not been groomed for some time. It could be weeks, it could be months. The dog itself is usually of limited importance to the household; often it spends most of its time out in the yard, apart from being fed and watered, receiving only minimal attention from its owners until somebody notices it smells bad, whereupon they call the kennel.

   There are also times when the question of grooming is governed by finances. Some people sacrifice to afford the luxury of having their pets groomed. Perhaps under the circumstances they shouldn't own a dog—but they do, and that's that.

2. **Personal pride.** Many owners get personal satisfaction from seeing their pet looking nice. In most cases the dog's role in the home is one of major significance—a love object or child substitute, perhaps. Carefully cultivated, this type of customer is money in the bank every four to six weeks, depending on how affluent he or she happens to be.

3. **A combination of the above.** This group probably comprises the majority of dog owners. They like their pets well enough but don't always get around to having them groomed regularly. Nice, well-meaning, good-natured people who sometimes let things slide a little longer than intended.

As the degree of emotional attachment and consequently the general attitude toward a pet varies considerably, each group must be handled differently. Regardless of anything else, trampling people's self-esteem into the ground is not the way to go.

Customer loyalty can never be taken for granted. Little things can cause them to switch. A kennel may open in a more convenient location. He or she may come to feel that you are not concerned enough about their individual preferences. Your hours may not be as accommodating as another operation's. (In large cities it is thought advisable to open earlier and close later than shops in a rural area. Many people like to drop off their dogs on the way to work and collect them on the way home that evening.) Your facility may be in need of a facelift or paint job. Whatever the reason, a loss of business means a loss of money. You are the one who suffers most.

Incidentally, customers' attitudes vary according to the socioeconomic and cultural area in which your business is located. Some people, regardless of what you do to please them, will still shop around looking for a better deal until they've tried every kennel or grooming shop in the area. Eventually they may settle on one for awhile, but chances are that they will continue to make the rounds ad infinitum.

The basic rule of thumb for a successful operation is to give customers what they want and are willing to pay for. The "we don't do that here" attitude is best kept for only the most drastic situations. After all, customers are used to being spoiled and pampered by the rest of the business community. They have come to believe that they're the boss—and like it or not they are.

Knowing how to manipulate customers is a terrific asset in business and can make your relationship with "the boss" more financially rewarding.

Know Your Customers

For many years leading companies have been trying to establish what separates top sales people from mediocre ones. It has been demonstrated that selling is a people problem and not an economic or technological one.

For example, in an era of great technological advances it is assumed that sales people with an appropriate engineering or technical background would have an advantage, but most businesses it seems are not technically oriented but are people oriented.

This has prompted a number of companies engaged in developing sales training techniques to develop systems variously called consultative selling, customer-oriented selling and life-style or behavioral selling.

Customer-oriented selling works by zeroing in on the customer's immediate economic needs; behavior or life-style selling is based on a different approach. Marketing and management-consulting firms that teach both consider life-style selling the most productive and by far the most interesting. Both methods are based on identifying four main types of customer personalities and tailoring the approach to fit individual needs.

The various personalities, recognized by the customer's speech, mannerisms and other indications, are:

1. **The Driver.** This type of customer is one who has to be in charge. He or she wants to get to the point, and looks the salesperson in the eye. This type is inclined to be an adventurous shopper. For the best results the salesperson must be logical, efficient and quick to suggest possible options but must avoid getting personal or emotional.

2. **The Expressor.** This customer needs recognition of his or her importance, and is likely to be excitable and a bit dramatic. Expressors use expressions and body movements freely. The sales person should refrain from pushing the expressor for a decision, and focus on being a good listener.

3. **The Amiable Customer.** This customer wants to be accepted by everyone and does not seem eager to get down to business. Usually, this customer sits back and looks relaxed. A sales person is required to be patient and cultivate a relationship—getting the customer more interested in him or her than in what's being sold.

4. **The Analytical Type.** This customer demands a great deal of patience, wants concise, accurate information and ample data to back each claim. Analyticals tend to speak slowly, stick to the facts and are generally sticklers for punctuality. They show little emotion and often avoid eye contact.

Take into consideration what the customer wants, what the customer needs and what the customer can afford—or is willing to pay for—at the same time catering to his or her personality, and you'll find selling much easier than you thought. This applies to both services and merchandise.

11

Making the Right Impression

PUBLIC RELATIONS—PR as it's called by the sophisticates of the business world—is the process of establishing understanding and good will between interested parties. Basically, it's another name for favorable advertising: the art of influencing people's opinions in favor of a particular person, product or, in the case of the kennel operator, service.

Most politicians as well as many celebrities employ high-powered PR men to keep their names before the public, as do major manufacturing and retail companies. The approach used is usually the subject of much consideration, discussion and sometimes extensive research before selecting the precise method to be employed in bringing something to the attention of the general public.

The old adage that says there is no such thing as bad publicity should not be taken as gospel, however.

Most advertising copy is geared to the premise that everyone wants to get the most value from every dollar. While there are laws governing truth in advertising that curb totally false statements and misleading claims, the truth can still be manipulated. The trick is to suggest or imply that products are more than they really are without telling an outright lie. TV ads for children's toys are a perfect example of how performance capabilities can be exaggerated by using clever production techniques. Another popular gimmick is having someone express a favorable opinion: "I believe it works best. . . ."

Sales pitches are tied to key "buzz words" or phrases that subconsciously trigger a favorable reaction or association by stressing the most appealing aspect of a product: "controls bad breath"; "relieves headache pain, fast"; ". . . for less"; "safer"; "more economical!" Secondary inducements are also emphasized: "better for your family"; "doctor recommended"; "used by more people."

Idea implants may be incorporated in the name of the product or the company (Thriftier Drugs, Jones' Discount Furniture) to create favorable mental pictures and ring those familiar bells to which we have been conditioned to respond as predictably as Pavlov's dog.

Your Business Name

Developing a favorable image starts the moment you first display your business name in public. For that reason alone the name you select should convey the type and quality of the services you're offering. Avoid subtleties. There is a danger of being too clever for your own good. Remember you are in business to make a living. That should always predominate your thinking and motivate your actions.

Some of the nation's major companies select new names for their products by computer. When a survey showed that many people thought that City Services was a branch of the Public Highways Department, the company changed its name to Citco from a list compiled by a computer, and then spent several million dollars advertising its new image to the buying public. This worked so well that other companies adopted the same idea.

The selection of a good business name is of utmost importance. It should not depend on what you like or what you think is smart or cute but on what the name will convey to your potential customers. The true meaning or dictionary definition of a word or name is rarely as important as what the average customer thinks it means. "Animal Clinic," for instance, conjures up an in-one-door-and-out-the-other impression while "Animal Hospital" opens up the possibility of hospitalization—which may be less acceptable to some people. "Pedigree Poodle Grooming" may convey the idea that you groom only pedigreed Poodles. "Le Petit Chien" sounds very French but what does it mean, and how many average people can pronounce it correctly? There are those who would be embarrassed to call a business with a name they couldn't pronounce. If customers keep asking, "Is this the place where you take care of dogs?" instead of referring to you by your business name, that could be a hint. For attracting the attention of the novice dog owner, most of whom seem to know little or nothing about boarding, grooming or related matters, fancy names may prove counterproductive. In choosing a name for your new business, keep it simple and explicit. "Pete's Dog Grooming Shop" beats the heck out of "Pierre's Boutique du Chien" unless you live in France or parts of Canada.

Slogans and sayings are of questionable merit unless they are fully understood by your potential clientele. Zero in on those you want to reach without beating around the bush. "We have warm hearts for cold noses" does not strike me as being as persuasive as, "We are pet-care experts." Some people may disagree, however.

Surprisingly, many people don't understand the difference between grooming and clipping. How many times have kennels been called by people who want them to "cut their dog," who need just a "Poodle cut" or who don't want their dog "shaved"? This indicates that not enough information is reaching the customer.

Advertising

Yellow Page advertising is unquestionably the most popular form of business advertising. Millions of dollars have been spent over the years telling us to "let our fingers do the walking" and it worked. Fortunately, as a result of pressure by the ABKA, kennel owners can now advertise all their services under one heading. Not so long ago boarding, grooming and other pet-related services were listed separately; that doubled and sometimes tripled the cost of advertising in this popular reference source.

Classified and newspaper display ads are the next most frequently used form of advertising. The basis of an effective display ad is not how much information you can cram into the least amount of space, but how much you can convey to readers in as few words as possible. Good advertising is never too crammed for easy reading. Your name, the services offered, your address and telephone number and maybe some eye-catching artwork are usually sufficient.

Good artwork is hard to find and it pays to be original. Therefore you may need the services of a commercial artist. As the majority of pet owners shun the idea of "show clips," displaying a simple photo or line drawing is the best middle-of-the-road approach. This applies equally to business cards and display advertising.

A humorous approach is not always appreciated. New dog owners don't seem to have much of a sense of humor. They take themselves very seriously and expect you to do likewise. I'm not keen on lots of schmaltz either, but that becomes a matter of personal preference and, as we all know, tastes differ a great deal.

Your Telephone Manner

The next important aspect of your image building is how you answer the telephone. If the phone rings, your ad has done its job. You must capitalize on that by reinforcing the favorable impression that prompted the call in the first place. Make the caller feel at ease. Simple telephone etiquette requires that you start by stating your business name and then your own: "Hello, Country Kennels and Grooming Shop . . . Jane speaking." From the customer's viewpoint there's a certain reassurance in knowing that he or she reached the right number. It saves having to ask.

Your telephone voice should be pleasant and not patronizing. If you sound gruff, curt or aggressive the caller may become defensive and difficult to reach. When you sound like a nice person, people will think you are a nice person.

A good sales pitch is important. Don't ad lib. Write down what you have to say and rehearse it thoroughly. Eventually you will develop your own particular dialogue. Use a tape recorder so you can hear yourself the way others will hear you. Sometimes that can be a jolt.

An authoritative, understated response to questions reflects an air of confidence and credibility. Speak slowly and distinctly and don't swamp the caller with irrelevancies. What the caller needs is a combination of information and reassurance. If you stammer and stutter, most people will assume you are less competent than you are.

Don't make sweeping statements or claims that won't hold up. Customers may hold you to your word and feel cheated if you cannot deliver. Talk in generalities and averages: "Boarding fees for medium dogs usually are. . . ."; "The normal charge for grooming the average Miniature Poodle is. . . ." Some callers are tricky, so don't commit yourself until you see the dog. The owner's idea of big, small, good or bad rarely coincides with the facts.

When you make appointments, ask for the caller's telephone number. There are at least two reasons for doing so: (1) if you need to cancel or change the appointment you will have the number, (2) the customer is no longer hidden in anonymity and therefore is less likely to disregard the appointment.

Your Personal Impression

When a customer walks through the door, you can strengthen or weaken the link between you by your appearance, your demeanor and your attitude toward his or her pet. If the dog looks like a potential troublemaker, encourage the owner to leave before trying to handle it. If the dog makes a fuss in front of its owner, say something like: "He doesn't want to leave you. But don't worry, he'll settle down when you leave and he'll be just fine." Smile when you say that.

Mailing grooming appointment reminders several days in advance and following that up with a phone call the day before the appointment encourages customers to keep their appointments. Some may find that a bit pushy. A lot depends on the people you are dealing with.

A gimmick that rarely fails to impress is sending holiday and birthday greeting cards to your canine client in care of its owner. For a little extra punch you can also include a Polaroid shot taken after a previous grooming and filed away for the occasion. That sort of thing takes time and may cost a few cents but don't view that as public relations. Think of it as insurance—insurance against losing out to a shrewder operator.

Lastly, refer all medical problems to one of your local veterinarians. Don't hesitate to let them know you are doing so. Build up an atmosphere of mutual trust and respect. That is also good public relations.

Enhancing Your Business Image

In many areas of the country business drops off to a minimum during the wintertime. So, instead of sitting around bemoaning the fact that you don't have much to do, why not use the time productively by decorating and brightening up your surroundings with a coat of fresh paint? A light, bright, newly painted office has an uplifting effect on one's morale. This applies both to kennel workers and their customers, and don't think that your customers won't notice and appreciate it.

If you've never tried your hand at painting before don't let that stop you. The new quick-drying, easy-to-apply, washable interior latex paints are a breeze to use. They come in a wide variety of pleasing colors. Light, warm yellows and oranges are more relaxing than the colder blues and greens. Stay away from dark colors. While these may appeal to some for reasons of practicality, dark colors absorb far too much light, which could contribute to eye strain by the end of a long working day. Similarly, avoid using too much bright white, which creates glare and may also cause eye strain. A matte or velvet finish will help to reduce glare to some extent.

A clean, tidy reception area reflects efficiency. Like it or not, it's all part of your image. Some of us are negligent in this department. Being good at your job is important, but looking the part is equally important. Most of us start off with a nicely painted facility but as time goes by we fail to realize that wear and tear has taken its toll. It would be a good policy to redecorate every year if you possibly can.

What people see as they pass can make either a good or bad impression on them. Even those who never enter your kennel can and do form an idea of how desirable it would be to leave their pet there. If they don't have a dog of their own their opinion could influence a friend or relative who has a pet and is looking for somewhere to take it. The outside appearance of your business should attract new customers as well as be appealing to your present ones. Inside, the fixtures, layout and displays should create an atmosphere in which the customer feels at home. Pet owners need to feel that their pride-and-joy is with a friend, a friend they can trust.

There is no doubt that the layout and decor reinforces the customer's impressions about you and your ability. Consider, also, the type of customer that you are hoping to attract. Heavy, solid fixtures of established design usually appeal to older and more conservative individuals. Plain, inexpensive-looking fixtures help younger people, whose income is often limited, relate to you. Ultracontemporary design appeals to the young and affluent. Low ceilings make your office seem more intimate and indirect lighting makes customers aware that you are concerned with quality. This all boils down to "atmosphere."

The impression you create, your image, is a major factor in determining the type of people you attract. If you already have a profitable business established with one segment of the community, it would be unwise to revamp your operation in the hope of attracting new clients from other walks of life.

An image is a complex thing and you should not try to change an already successful one without much thought and careful planning. Ask yourself these questions: What kind of image do I have now? What kind of image do I want? How can I improve my image and is it necessary? No one can answer those questions for you. In the long haul, your image is your own responsibility.

12

Good Public Relations

WILL ROGERS IS often quoted as saying, "I never met a man I didn't like." Assuming that "man" in this particular context was used as a neuter pronoun, he obviously felt the same way about women. It certainly sounds like a warm, benevolent sentiment, expressed by a kind, understanding person. Frankly, I suspect that Will was not being totally sincere, but it was a great line that certainly did nothing to harm his own popularity. If Will Rogers were alive today he would probably have to reconsider that statement.

Generally speaking, most pet-care professionals are basically nice people. However, some obviously fail to grasp the basic principals of making a favorable impression on others, and consequently present themselves in an unfavorable light. They just don't interrelate successfully.

It is fairly safe to assume that we all want to be liked. It is also a fact that, unlike Mr. Rogers, we will encounter people whom we dislike and vice versa. The truth is that most of us are both likable and not so likable, depending on the circumstances. Sometimes we change our opinions about people who may have created a bad initial impression on us after we have a chance to get to know them better. Sometimes we don't.

Getting Customers' Confidence

According to psychological studies, the more we like ourselves the more we are liked by others. This does not necessarily apply to your neighborhood egomaniac who forces himself and his opinions down everyone's throat. Respect also plays a significant part in most relationships. You cannot like somebody you do not respect.

In a business where competition is plentiful, projecting a likable image can make a considerable difference to one's income. Businesswise, it is generally better for a customer to like you for yourself than for the quality of your work. This is important because most of us find it difficult to trust people we don't like, and kennel management involves gaining trust.

First impressions always play a big part in the way others relate to us. The telephone is the most frequent method of initial contact with a prospective client. Kennel owners and managers who want to get the most out of their Yellow Page or other advertising should pay particular attention to this aspect of communication. A phone conversation with a prospective customer should be conducted with the knowledge that the caller will, in his or her own mind, determine a great deal about your character in terms of being nice, kind, cruel, pleasant, unpleasant, calm, agitated, tense, strong, weak, knowledgeable or otherwise by the way you talk to them on the telephone.

Good telephone-answering technique is an acquired skill. One must say just enough to satisfy the caller without volunteering any unessential information that might prove counterproductive. A curt reply that does not answer questions the caller may feel are important may instill an element of doubt as to your sensitivity to his or her needs or his or her pet.

A low, calm voice with a controlled speech pattern and with a warm, friendly attitude usually makes the best impression. A breathless, stammering, obviously agitated individual does not promote confidence, nor does gruffness or rudeness for that matter.

Prospective customers need plenty of reassurance. Your job is to help dispel their misgivings, not add to them. One way to do this is to always be as helpful as possible. If you don't have enough time to spend talking to potential customers on the phone, then you must make arrangements for someone else to take the calls. Customers should never be made to feel that they are not worth a little of your time. That's a putdown that most of them will resent. Put yourself in the other person's shoes. Would you give your business to someone who snubbed you over the phone? Hardly!

Chaotic background noises also contribute to an unfavorable impression. During a survey I did several years ago I found that it was almost impossible to conduct any sort of intelligible telephone conversation with many kennel and grooming shop owners because of the racket going on in the background. There were dryers and clippers running, dogs barking and, in several instances, people yelling at either the dogs or each other.

In most areas the telephone company has an attachment available called a confidencer that will reduce many of the extraneous background noises that callers might otherwise hear. The average monthly rental for a confidencer works out at around one dollar, plus a one-time installation fee. Every grooming shop and kennel phone should be equipped with a confidencer. There's probably no better business investment you can make for the price.

Finally, don't let children answer the phone; use an answering device instead. When people call a business number they expect to speak with an adult who is both willing and able to answer their questions. Allowing children to answer the phone raises doubts about just how business-like your operation is.

After you have charmed a new customer into your kennel it is necessary to reinforce the good impression you made over the phone. It's no good being "Mr. or Miss Wonderful" on the telephone and behaving like a bear with a sore head once the customer arrives. Regardless of your personal trials and tribulations, customers are entitled to consideration and courtesy. They should not become involved in your problems unless their dog is one of the contributing factors. Most people don't want to hear your tales of woe. They have their own setbacks to contend with. So, be nice. Don't unload on your customers.

We are all creatures of habit. If we let ourselves behave badly it will soon become second nature to us. If we try to be nice all the time we may forget how to be anything else. And while customers may generally be on the fickle side, they are far less likely to look elsewhere once you have made them feel that they are important to you, and they are. Without customers there's no point to staying in business.

If you are not sure about the way you come across when dealing with the general public, try running a tape recorder in your shop for just one day. It may open both your eyes and your ears to hear how you sound to others.

In addition to everything else, it is important to listen to what the customer has to say. Under normal circumstances, the average person grasps only about twenty-five percent of what you tell them—if they are paying attention. If you allow yourself to be distracted, which is easy enough to do, you may fail to fully understand all the instructions you are given. Concentrate on what the speaker is saying, and make notes so that you can refresh your memory later in the day when you have to deal with that particular dog. Do not depend on your memory alone—that's how mistakes occur.

Being successful in the pet-care business involves more than knowing how to handle dogs. It also involves knowing how to attract and keep customers and how to make a lasting impression. It involves making people like you. That is salesmanship, and anyone who is both a good kennel operator and a good salesman will never have much to worry about. Good PR is money in the bank.

Special Promotions

Caroline C. Roden and Lois Preston, owners of the Preston Country Club for Pets, a full-service facility in Columbia, Maryland, accepted the opportunity to participate in a local Chamber of Commerce business fair. This is Caroline Roden's version of what happened, as it appeared in *Petcare Professional Magazine*:

It started when we received a letter from our local Chamber of Commerce asking members to participate in an exhibit to be held in March at a large shopping mall three miles from our kennel and grooming shop. After talking to the Pennsylvania Groomers' Associations, who had previously done mall exhibits, and receiving some very positive feedback, we decided to go ahead, rent a booth and put on a three-day promotion.

The 8' × 10' booth came draped with red and white satin. We decorated it with silhouettes of dogs interspersed with enlarged black and white photos of our facilities, brought in a raised platform and grooming table, and conducted continuous grooming demonstrations.

The public's enthusiasm exceeded all expectations. Thousands of people stopped by the booth to watch, pick up our brochure which was prominently displayed, ask questions, and help themselves to the various pet-care pamphlets and free samples. We had a videotape on dog grooming on loan from Oster, and a daily free drawing for a bath and trim. We drew the biggest crowds in the show, and subsequently received the Chamber's Award of Excellence for our display. We were told that we'd be given a more strategic location next time so that we don't block traffic. It was great fun and good publicity. At a total cost of around $400 (including lost income from grooming), it was the most successful promotion we have ever done. The phone rang constantly during and after the show, and many who called are now booking into the shop and kennel. We had 450 registrations for the free trim drawings, and we then used this list of people who had seen our work for other promotions.

The demonstrations included Poodles in different trims, Panda cuts on various breeds, terriers, a Cocker, a Bouvier des Flandres, a St. Bernard, an Afghan, a Maltese and a Yorkshire Terrier (the last three were groomed, bathed and cage-dried in advance, then wet down and blow-dried at the show). The "people pleaser" was the dual grooming of the 200 lb. St. Bernard on the floor and the tiny Yorkie on the table. Grooming the Bouvier brought dozens of inquiries about the breed, which prompted us to attach a hastily written sign to the grooming table within a few minutes.

When we began organizing for the show, we selectively booked in the dog models for regular grooming appointments with the understanding that they would be transported to the mall for finishing after bathing and fluffing at the shop. The dogs to be done in the late evening were picked up that day, groomed, kept overnight, and delivered the next day with only a grooming charge. We conservatively booked six to seven dogs per day, but ran out of dogs at the booth. We could have handled one an hour, which would also have helped reduce the cost of the show. Many proud owners watched from a

This highly successful mall promotion was conducted by the owners and staff of the Preston Country Club.

An overhead view of the layout of the Preston Country Club booth.

POOCH PALACE DOG BOARDING & GROOMING

(your pet's home away from home)

ALL BREEDS EXPERTLY GROOMED BY APPOINTMENT

2000 W. Your St.

Anywhere, USA 00000

CALL: 999-5555

| 999-5555 |
| 999-5555 |
| 999-5555 |
| 999-5555 |
| 999-5555 |
| 999-5555 |
| 999-5555 |
| 999-5555 |
| 999-5555 |
| 999-5555 |
| 999-5555 |
| 999-5555 |
| 999-5555 |
| 999-5555 |
| 999-5555 |
| 999-5555 |
| 999-5555 |
| 999-5555 |
| 999-5555 |
| 999-5555 |
| 999-5555 |
| 999-5555 |

Sample Notice.

Standard 5 M 5 in. file card. Perforate along the dotted line and cut along the vertical lines between phone numbers to allow easy removal.

vantage point on the upper level of the mall, where their pets could not see them, and they loved it!

In order to have all-day coverage, our three groomers worked staggered shifts, one starting at 7:30 A.M., one at 9, and the third at 11. There was usually one groomer at the shop getting dogs ready, one in transit, and one at the booth. We didn't crate the dogs as there was always at least one other person at the booth to hold them. The spectators enjoyed getting a close look at the finished dogs so much that we kept one available for that purpose.

We were not without problems. One being that after a winter's neglect we needed more dematting time than we had estimated and it was not easy getting the dogs to the booth on schedule. Next time we plan to have some dogs in the day before ready to go.

At night the lighting was poor. Supplemental lighting helped, but not enough for dark dogs. The solution is to schedule white ones at night. This would have helped another problem. The sun was so bright that we were blinded by the white dogs during the day. Lastly, overenthusiastic spectators constantly pushed the booth into disarray. Next time I plan to wedge something heavy against the table legs to keep them steadier.

We were extremely happy with the way the show went. In addition to the business generated, our groomers developed a renewed sense of pride in their craft.

Profitable "Free" Advertising

Every year kennel operators spend a substantial amount of money paying for various forms of advertising to promote their kennels and grooming shops, a considerable part of which is allocated to the Yellow Pages. Unfortunately, it is only possible to contract for Yellow Page listings once a year. This means that anyone starting a new business may have to wait up to a full year before getting any benefit from this particular form of advertising.

An excellent way of getting additional free publicity is to post notices on bulletin boards in supermarkets, post offices, shopping centers, laundromats, office buildings, apartment complexes, beauty shops, feed stores and veterinary hospitals.

Notices can be typed or printed either on 5 × 8 in. index cards or half sheets of plain typing paper. The amount of information should be kept to a minimum. Most people are not going to spend time reading a lot of superfluous copy, so keep it short and to the point (see sample).

To make it convenient for prospective customers to take home your telephone number, write or type it vertically across the bottom of your card as shown. Perforate above the numbers, as indicated by the dotted line, either with a needle or by running the card through an unthreaded sewing machine. Separate them by cutting along the solid lines so that individual strips can easily be torn off without destroying the notice itself.

Even if you already have advertisements appearing elsewhere, spreading these notices around in strategic locations is bound to stimulate additional business.

13

What's Your Sign?

DRIVING ALONG ONE of the main highways I frequently travel going from one town to the next, I noticed a particular grooming shop sign for the first time. It was tasteful enough, I suppose. The problem is that I had driven past it for a year or more without seeing it before.

The Effective Sign

A sign should not be just a location marker but a 24-hour-a-day advertising campaign. Signs need not be expensive or elaborate to be effective. In fact, they are often more noticeable when kept as simple as possible. Too many kennel owners, and others, are guilty of either skimping on signs or being too "artistic" for their own good.

Two important things to remember are that a sign must have both readability and durability.

The effectiveness of any sign is governed, in part, by the speed of passing traffic and whether it is placed at right angle to or parallel with the highway. The driver of a car traveling at 50 miles per hour has up to 40 seconds to read a sign placed at a right angle to the highway; depending on its size and clarity, that's the approximate amount of time it will be in focus for the average person.

A sign placed parallel with the highway, like one on the front of a building, which stands back less than 20 feet from the road, may be visible for only five seconds to the driver of a vehicle traveling 30 miles per hour. Most drivers will see it peripherally as they drive by, if at all. They may not

The original bland Tri City Animal Care Center sign on the left was replaced by the modern illuminated version on the right.

A bench sign leased by Master Grooming of Chicago. This is a great way to get your message to potential customers.

have a chance to take their eyes off the traffic ahead of them. It is a distinct advantage to have your sign located close to a stop sign or intersection where traffic is forced to reduce speed or stop.

Cost and Impact

Signs may cost from 50 to several hundred dollars each. The thing to remember is: if people can't read them, they're not worth a dime.

Generally speaking, the best sign has clear, uncrowded black lettering on a plain white background. Fancy, ornate, or multicolored lettering is more difficult to read from a moving vehicle.

If investing money erecting an expensive sign, one presumes you would like it to last as long as possible. Colored signs, especially blue, red and yellow tend to fade quickly in full sun. Plain black and white holds up best of all.

Signs need a minimum of information: name and type of business, location and phone number. Too much body copy obscures the message.

In certain areas of the country, you can have your message written on benches placed at strategic locations, such as bus stops, etc., which can also be seen by passing travelers. The same rule of thumb applies to these as to other signs. Keep the copy brief—name, type of business and its location. These benches are also frequently used to indicate the advertiser's location at intersections.

Advertising is an important part of every business venture. The cost of advertising is increasing rapidly; don't waste the opportunity of getting your message to prospective customers by the cheapest method of all: an attractive, well-placed sign outside your kennel.

14

Paying Your Way

IN THE 1980s many pet-care operators experienced their best years ever. Unfortunately, during the same timeframe an unprecedented number of small businesses passed into oblivion—twice as many as in previous years. Economists unanimously predict that radical changes in our way of life are just around the corner, as the value of a dollar is shrinking at an alarming rate. In order to survive the money crunch we must make some important adjustments, not the least of which is learning how to budget our income and handle our money more efficiently than ever before.

Most major distributors have the same complaint: customers don't pay their bills on time, if at all. This results in the eventual loss of credit, not just for primary offenders but for everyone in general.

No one has any idea just what will happen in the future. Perhaps the best safeguard is to anticipate the worst. For this reason it is important to take time to evaluate one's assets and liabilities realistically.

The Wise Uses of Credit

An essential step in the right direction is keeping out of debt. Overutilization of credit often leads to bankruptcy. Many would-be experts are advising people to borrow as much as they can, based on the presumption that they will eventually be paying off their debts in cheaper dollars. This principle is better in theory than fact. Those who get too deeply in debt are unlikely to survive long enough to put that idea into practice.

To protect themselves against customers who are not credit worthy, manufacturers and distributors are compiling lists of potential "bad risks," so it will soon become almost impossible for deadbeats to run up sizable debts with every distributor in the area. Without essential supplies it is impossible to function.

To maintain a healthy industry everyone must pay their debts. It's impossible to do that if you are continually hitting the cash register. For many operators, cash is the number-one problem—not too little, too convenient. Cash in hand is too spendable. All income should be banked, but in many cases those very negotiable dollar bills go from the cashbox to the pocketbook. That is where most money problems start. What actually goes into the bank may not be enough to pay those pesky overheads, and once cash has been spent it's gone forever.

Obtaining Credit

As many kennel operators are women, they should be aware of the Equal Credit Opportunity Act of 1975, which prohibits credit discrimination on a variety of grounds, including gender. There are several other legislative acts in place that serve to protect loan seekers. The Fair Credit Reporting Act regulates the credit-reporting agencies that provide information to creditors about consumers. The Truth in Lending Act requires lenders to disclose the cost of credit in understandable terms. The Fair Credit Billing Act forces creditors to resolve billing disputes within a reasonable timeframe. The Fair Debt Collection Act prevents the use of unduly abrasive or abusive debt collection tactics by collection agencies.

With bank credit tough to find, many individuals are looking to finance companies for help. Banks generally regard finance company borrowers as bad risks because the widely used computerized credit-scoring system used by banks assigns a low rating to former finance company clients.

The best rule is to rely on credit only when necessary. Buy only what you need, not what you think you'd like. Credit is a business tool: always use it wisely.

Gross Income and Net Profit

At one point I learned from a distributor that eighteen of twenty apparently successful businesses had suddenly failed. Obviously they had not been doing as well as it seemed.

One incident is worth recounting. It involved an eager new owner of a franchised pet shop. During his first, second, third and fourth weeks in business his store had set consecutive sales records for a new shop with the franchise. Imagine his disillusionment when at the end of the month, instead of the fantastic profit he had anticipated he actually lost money. In fact, it is doubtful that he ever managed to break even. After several devastating months he was forced to give up the business. It was a classical example of being lulled into believing that an impressive *gross income* automatically reflected a healthy *net profit*.

Net profit is the most important indicator of the success of any business operation and we should all be concerned about the reliability of that figure. There are several ways in which profit can be erroneously stated. Basic to accurate profit determination is a system of accurate and meaningful accounting. The words *accurate* and *meaningful* are significant, because not all accounting systems convey a realistic picture of the results of an operation. While the proper mechanics of accounting may assure a balancing of debts and credits, this procedure will not of itself tell the whole profit story. Such information must be interpreted to provide the owner with a sound basis on which to conduct future business operations. Computerization can help you do this more efficiently.

Certainly, consideration of the accounting procedures is necessary since a figure of net profit has to be derived from some system. However, the detailed procedure of bookkeeping itself is of far less interest than the method by which it is applied to business policy.

There are three major areas in which you can fool yourself about your profits: (1) the existence of a profit, (2) the sufficiency of the profit, and (3) the profit trend.

Is There a Profit?

The first question to ask is, Do I actually have a *real profit*? It must be realized that a final answer to this question is not necessarily indicated by the figure of "net profit" shown on the profit-and-loss (P & L) statement. To be certain that you are not being misled by this figure, you must analyze the basis of it carefully.

An orderly procedure is to start at the top of the P & L statement and compare it, item by item, with several other operating periods. Try to evaluate the meanings of any changing trends that could transform profit into loss.

There are two principal methods of reporting income and expenses on the P & L statement: the Cash Method and the Accrual Method. Many use the Cash Method, which shows only the actual receipt of cash (income) and the actual expenditures of cash (expenses). The Accrual Method reflects business transactions that took place during the reporting period whether or not money changed hands. These two methods can convey totally different profit pictures.

The Cash Method is accurate only if no credit business was conducted during the reporting period. This is often the case with kennels and grooming establishments.

You might want to discuss your specific business requirements with a qualified accountant.

Sales: Some accounting procedures do not go to the extent of determining net sales (generally the gross sales, less returns and allowances). Make sure that the sales figures reflect the actual final sales that took place in the period covered by the P & L.

Cost of goods sold and inventory valuation: The cost of goods sold, the next item after net sales on the P & L, is determined by subtracting the inventory at the end of the period from the total obtained by adding the inventory at the beginning of the period to purchases made during the period. *Note:* Beginning inventory purchases are often referred to as "merchandise available for sale." Sometimes this method of inventory valuation can be the cause of significant distortion in the profit picture. If the closing inventory was valued high, for instance, the cost of goods sold would be lower and profits higher. Thus, the cost of goods sold figure can be distorted by changes in the method of inventory valuation or by failure to observe sound valuation methods.

Each operator should review his or her own inventory procedures to determine what basis is used and if this basis reflects the most realistic value of the stock on hand.

One of the critical areas in over- or understatement of profits is that of depreciation. This is a specific area where you can be misled by what appears to be a sound and accurate accounting procedure. For one thing, the depreciation account can show a record of depreciation down to the exact penny. Entries in this account give the impression of absolute accuracy. Because of this you can easily lose sight of the fact that the human judgment that established the original depreciation rate could have been in error—sometimes in gross error.

By way of illustration, the decision to depreciate store fixtures over a period of ten years, made by a kennel owner, proved to be unrealistic when it was found that these items reached the limits of their usefulness and needed to be replaced after six years. So, for six years the owner fooled himself about his profit.

Review depreciation policies in terms of your past experience, good judgment and business trends in the trade. The tax rules of the Internal Revenue Service inform you of legal limitations and serve as a basis for a realistic depreciation policy and can be a useful guide. However, in new situations it is often desirable to establish depreciation schedules through detailed discussions with Internal Revenue authorities or business consultants as to what is reasonable in your particular case.

In addition to making your depreciation policies realistic, you also should determine whether all depreciable items are included in your depreciation schedules.

Owners mislead themselves about monthly profits when they do not take into account charges and expenses that only occur annually. In many smaller businesses these items are not considered until they arise at the end of the year—often to the disillusionment of the owners. Such omissions are particularly noticeable in job-cost estimations. The proprietor thinks he is figuring jobs on the basis of a good profit but finds that his total operating expenses should have included a number of things he failed to consider in the day-to-day job estimations. Some examples of these are income taxes, insurance premiums and rent (if paid quarterly or annually).

Another expense allied to the annual and quarterly expenses is that for facilities and equipment maintenance. The monthly P & L statement may fail to carry an allowance for this expense for some months. In that case the profits for those months will have to be readjusted when repair bills fall due. Sometimes these bills can be large enough to wipe out a percentage of the profits.

Is the Profit Sufficient?

Many businesses that appear to be making a reasonable profit would find a changed situation if they allowed a comfortable salary for the owner-operator. Often the proprietor draws money out of the business on an irregular basis, as needed. Often this does not amount to reasonable compensation when compared with the pay of others working on a regular salary or commission basis.

For example, if total withdrawals for a year were made by an owner-operator to the tune of $5,000 when the going pay scale for comparable work was in the $10,000 range, a supposed profit of $5,000 would be the direct result of the owner being underpaid by that amount. If someone was hired to perform the same duties at an appropriate salary the alleged profit would become nonexistent.

The profit figure can also contain amounts that are the result of unjustifiable risk-taking by the management. Serious fires, or other potential disasters, if not covered by sufficient insurance protection could cause a drain on company resources that would wipe out much or all of the profits for a given year. When a businessman does not carry adequate protection against such disasters, somewhat more profit will be shown each month. In such instances the profit figure is at least partly due to false savings brought about by undue risk-taking.

How much protection is "adequate" is a matter of judgment. For the best advice consult your insurance agent, company representative or your banker.

With the current emphasis on compliance with minimum wage laws it is increasingly important for everyone to clarify the status of their kennel in this regard. Make sure you are not projecting inflated profits by paying employees less than required by law. If caught paying below minimum wages you may be compelled to retroactively reimburse all employees. That would certainly put a crimp in your ledger.

Profit Trend

Once you determine that you have a profit, be sure you are not setting standards too low in comparison to others performing similar services. If you establish sound criteria your evaluations will be valid.

You may be satisfied with the existence and sufficiency of profit and still misjudge the profit trend. An examination of the profit picture at any given point in time may give a satisfactory impression. Viewed over the long haul, however, it might show undesirable trends: increased volume but declining net profit ratios, expenses growing disproportionately faster than the net profits.

It is essential for owners and managers to note significant fluctuations. One simple method of keeping track of things is to use an old-fashioned graph. While business fluctuations are bound to occur on a seasonal basis, irregular or unexpected downward shifts require frequent careful scrutiny. The remedy may be as simple as changing business hours or cutting back on the number of employees.

The preceding considerations are not intended to be all inclusive. Other factors may also be worth analyzing to determine profit trends. Using this guide, kennel owners should develop their own checklist of potential trouble spots.

Kennel operators are entitled to make an adequate return for their investment of time and money. Unless you do there is no point being in business. You are your own best asset. Don't sell yourself short. There are plenty of ways to establish the minimum charges needed to earn a respectable wage and show a reasonable profit.

Those without previous business experience may mistakenly consider their wages as "profit." Not so. Wages are payment for work performed. Profit is the "something extra" that remains after operating expenses—including your own wages—have been deducted from the gross income.

Advertising, telephone, rent or mortgage, lighting, heating, cooling, taxes, licensing, equipment costs, etc. all constitute business expenditures. Consumables, plant maintenance and depreciation must also be deducted from gross income to establish the total running costs of your particular operation. Dividing this amount by the number of dogs you board and groom on an annual basis gives you the average unit cost for each animal you handle.

Anyone going into business must quickly learn to differentiate between "gross" and "net" income. Gross is everything that flows through the cash register. Net is what's left after you settle all your commitments. Sometimes the two are a long way apart.

The most frequent cause of business failure comes from (1) being underfinanced and/or (2) treating gross income like net income and spending it for one's needs without realizing it belongs to your creditors.

The correct business procedure is to bank your gross, including the cash, and pay yourself a basic wage as you would any other employee. Utilizing the gross for personal use is fiscal suicide.

Anyone saying, "I made $100 today," probably means, "I grossed $100 today"; the two are not synonymous, obviously.

Those in business for themselves work for the world's most demanding employers. And why not; aren't you doing it for your own benefit? Maybe so, but are you getting what you are worth for that effort?

Being in business entitles you to make a reasonable profit as a reward for taking the risks involved in any venture. One way of computing it is to tally your overheads, including *your* wages, and add 25 percent. Expenses plus wages plus profit add up to a commercially sound business venture that allows you to pay your way.

One final note: Any individual or company that acquires an established business or substantially all the assets of a business becomes liable for all or any unpaid unemployment taxes owed by the seller. Check that out before you buy and avoid unpleasant surprises later.

15

Expand Your Business, Not Your Facility

DURING THE BUSY SEASON kennel owners may find that their boarding business is more than they can handle. Pets are boarded for up to several weeks while their owners are off having a good time, and you might find yourself turning new customers away to give priority to your regulars.

Enlarging your facility to relieve this seasonal overload would only necessitate the need to generate increased *nonseasonal* year-round business to match your added capacity. Survey the area within a reasonable radius. Do you see a potential for more business that would justify expansion?

If you have a known quantity of steady customers throughout the year you can be prepared for them, but to get new customers year-round you must promote year-round. They must always think of you when their pets need boarding, grooming or supplies.

Promotion

Educate the public about the products and services you offer. If your customers bring in their dogs only once a year, you must modify that behavior pattern through promotion.

Promotion can be divided into three broad categories: advertising, personal selling and sales promotion and publicity—which includes public relations. Each should be considered an essential part of the total promotional mix. Coordinating your efforts can create an effective promotional campaign designed to suit your own particular needs.

The first step in your promotional campaign is to establish your priorities. Without a goal to reach you cannot determine if the campaign is a success.

Next, determine whether an immediate or future response is most important. Should your promotional effort be geared only to annual or semiannual occasions (creating annual or semiannual customers) or do you intend to develop enduring customer support that will provide a source of steady income? While not ignoring the former, the latter would be the smart choice. Creating a steady flow of income throughout the year should be your primary objective. Developing long-term promotion is also important, even when you are number one in the area.

How much of a promotional budget should you allocate? There is no set rule for determining your promotional budget. The most popular method is to assign a percentage of the gross sales as the figure. Industry figures of the nation's largest advertisers range from 1 percent to over 30 percent of gross annual sales.

Once you have decided on your objective you should consider the various alternatives by which you can reach this goal. Increasing customers throughout the year means increasing the number of dog owners who are in a position to use the products and services you have to offer.

Using the Media

What is the most effective way of communicating with and educating prospective customers about your products and services? Let's review your media choices.

Newspapers can be divided into general categories, depending on size and readership. In metropolitan areas there is usually the major daily and the suburban or neighborhood newspaper—sometimes supplemented by a shoppers' guide, the content of which is primarily advertising. Smaller towns may have their own daily newspaper, similar in content to suburban papers, as well as a shoppers' guide. Others may have only weekly newspapers.

If your kennel is in a major metropolitan area, you may not find it profitable to advertise in the daily newspaper unless it also contained a section of particular interest to dog owners.

Television, while obviously effective as an advertising medium, is used primarily to reach a mass market and it would probably be too expensive for most pet-care businesses to consider.

Radio, on the other hand, should be investigated. Radio audiences are segmented by age, education, sex and income in relation to their listening habits. The station to choose would be one of the less expensive in the market. It should not be a top general audience station. The top stations appeal to the masses, your business does not.

In larger markets, especially on the FM band, listeners can be segmented geographically. If one of these stations saturates your area, see if it conveys the type of climate in which you would like to run your advertising.

The most selective medium you can use for advertising is direct mail. A well-designed flyer mailed to dog owners selected from the municipal dog license list should provide encouraging results. However, direct mail advertising is an art; to do it correctly might involve hiring a professional consultant.

Are you aware of the fact that at this moment you could have an advertisement working for you 24 hours a day? It's your outside kennel sign. The most simple outdoor sign can convey your message very effectively at minimum cost.

Is your sign a good one? If not it probably won't motivate anybody. Any promotional undertaking has got to make people look up and take notice.

All the promotional ideas discussed so far have been geared to attracting customers. The next step is to make them spend money with point-of-purchase displays to help increase your sales of certain items, combined with pushing sundry services on a low-key basis.

Whichever sales media you choose, use it consistently. A consistent message has a snowball effect.

Telling Your Story

Deciding where to tell your story is only one aspect of a successful ad campaign. You must tell an effective story. One that will sell. Promote yourself as a problem solver. Also offer goods and services that pet owners need and exploit that to the hilt. In addition, plan special promotions throughout the year to help bring in new customers.

For these promotions you can make use of special offers, premiums, contests and games. Get the people into your kennel or shop throughout the year and they'll bring you their dogs throughout the year.

It is essential to develop an image for your kennel or shop that will set it apart from the competition. Stress friendliness, professionalism and personal service, and build your promotions around that image.

Combined with the promotional mix concept is the use of publicity and public relations, important parts of which are press releases and community relations. The goal of public relations is to convey a favorable image of your place of business to the public through the use of highly credible sources, i.e., newspaper columnists, word-of-mouth, etc.

Essentially, you must create newsworthy events, from posting dog and cat lost-and-found signs in your local supermarket to holding free grooming clinics at your kennel. It is surprising how eager local papers are for news.

The main use of public relations should be to give people that "good feeling" when they think about you by making them believe you care about them. Implementing these ideas need not be expensive, especially if you concentrate on local media and design promotions personalized to your business.

Periodically evaluate the results of your campaign. If there are some weaknesses in the mix, strengthen or replace them with stronger ones. Be flexible; nothing works every time. Learn to discard a bad promotional idea that doesn't work.

There are numerous options with which to work and taking time to plan effective advertising is an important part of any successful business enterprise. After all, you don't really need a bigger business, you need a more profitable one. The two are not synonymous.

16

Capitalize on Impulse Buying

$\mathbf{B}$OOSTING PRICES at a time when customers are watching every dime may do more harm than good, since many people would compensate for increased prices by having their pets boarded and groomed less frequently. A more subtle approach would be to induce them to "voluntarily" spend more money by capitalizing on impulse buying.

Creative Merchandising

A sizable percentage of kennels offer no services to their customers except boarding and grooming. Many, understandably enough, feel that they don't have time to be bothered with merchandising, which can be a potential time-waster. However, approached correctly, merchandising on a limited basis can provide extra income with little or no effort.

Retail sales of certain products can be increased by stimulating impulse buying. To capitalize on this opportunity you must select merchandise with that end in mind. Goods offered as impulse items must be:

- What the customer wants or needs or thinks he wants or needs.
- Competitively priced compared to other outlets.
- Easily stored to minimize waste or damage.
- Consumable to ensure repeat sales.
- Normally used by the consumer and/or backed by aggressive national advertising (flea collars are a perfect example).

Like every other shopper the average pet owner routinely buys certain impulse items, usually from the supermarket. Flea collars, flea spray, chew toys, treats and vitamins come readily to mind. Why not cater to this predictable characteristic? Kennel owners who do not encourage their customers to buy from them, instead of taking their business to the supermarket, are missing a golden opportunity to boost their income because many people buy on the spur of the moment.

Your local supermarket provides a fine example of this type of behavior. A reliable estimate is that from 50 to 65 percent of all items bought in supermarkets are picked off the shelves on impulse. Customers do not plan to buy these products but do so on impulse.

Motivation for this type of buying starts at the factory with enticing packaging. Supermarkets and other alert retailers slant their promotional activities, especially their displays, to urge customers to buy, buy, buy. With a little thought you can make it just as easy for customers to do that in your shop or kennel.

What is meant by "impulse buying"? Some students of human behavior think of it as emotional, nonrational buying. Others view an impulse purchase as the result of a combination of psychological and economic factors. From the kennel owners' point of view, impulse buying means that the purchase was not preceded by a formal buying plan, i.e., the customer had no intention of buying the specific item in question when he or she first entered the building.

Certain goods, such as those mentioned earlier, go hand in hand with impulse buying. They are products that the customers want to buy on sight and which they may have bought many times before but which are relatively unimportant to their everyday lives. With a little timely prompting they will buy just as readily from you as from an alternative outlet. Sometimes they are motivated by brand preference, sometimes it's just the item itself. The relative factor is in the way the decision to purchase is reached.

When a customer buys an item with prior intent, it is considered a convenience item. When he or she buys the same thing on the spur of the moment it becomes an impulse item. We have all made impulse purchases in the supermarket, the drugstore or at a bargain counter. It may have been either a practical or frivolous purchase, motivated by a product display suggestion.

Much spur-of-the-moment buying is done because people tend to like a change periodically. They just want to try something new or different. The first step toward converting your customers to impulse buying is to carefully select the items that catch their eye and trigger that desire to buy.

Why people act as they do is a complex puzzle that psychologists and others are continually trying to solve, but you don't need to be an authority on what makes people tick in order to get them to buy. It is important to remember that many prospective customers don't realize that they want or need a certain item until they see it on display.

Impulse items should be priced for a quick turnover. Shopworn merchandise becomes progressively more difficult to move. So, not only should your display prompt the customer into buying, the items you are offering should be priced to sell. For the "average" person that means somewhere in the $4 to $5 range. An item priced at $4.95 usually sells better than one marked $5.

Your customer's knowledge and use of a product are also important considerations in selecting merchandise for impulse sales. The less selling needed, the quicker the decision to buy. For example, the strong national TV advertising campaign promoting the use of flea and tick collars has made this item one of the great "impulse" buys of all time. Chew-bones are another.

The trick is to sell your customers flea and tick collars before they buy them at their local supermarket. The most opportune time for that is immediately after they have had their pet groomed—especially if it arrived infested with fleas or ticks. This also applies to various other products. The best time to make your pitch is when the owner is demonstrating active concern for his or her pet's welfare because they are already emotionally attuned to doing something positive for the animal.

If clipping reveals a dry skin problem or that a dog is in apparently poor general condition, which might indicate a vitamin deficiency, you can mention this fact to the owner. Chances are that he or she will want to do whatever possible to correct the situation, whether that means taking the dog to a veterinarian or giving it extra vitamins. Several companies market attractively packaged vitamin products that make ideal impulse buying items. There is certainly nothing unethical in persuading a customer to buy from you instead of the store down the street. In fact, it shows you have good business sense.

Effective Displays

The final and most important step in merchandising impulse items is attracting the customer's eye. You have to direct the customers' attention toward the articles you want them to pick up and buy.

For the average kennel or grooming shop there are three things to remember: (1) an effective interior display, (2) the location of the display, and (3) point-of-purchase advertising.

Attractive interior displays help brighten your shop. Manufacturer-supplied displays are often available. These sales aids can help set the mood for impulse buying and are designed to show off the product in its most favorable light.

Sales displays must be located where the customer will have the opportunity to study them. The best place is on top of the counter in the area of the cash register. The impulse to buy seems to be greatest while they are in the act of paying for other goods or services or waiting to do so. Make your pitch—if you intend to make one—before the customer pays. If you have to make change, take your time so that he or she can deliberate on what you had to say.

Point-of-purchase advertising tells the customer about the merits of the goods. Such advertising, usually supplied by the manufacturer of the product in question, is sure to stress the product's most important selling point.

The amount of impulse selling you do is directly proportionate to the number of people that visit your place of business: the more traffic, the more sales. But in any event it's a little something extra and those little extras have a way of adding up over a period of time.

Subletting Selling Space

For kennel operators who positively do not want to be involved in retail merchandising, the answer may be to sublet retail space to someone who is interested in retail selling. As happens all too frequently, industrious individuals are held back because they lack starting capital. Here is one example of how that problem was solved by two imaginative individuals, as explained to me by Lynn Kittle:

Lynn left her job in a carpet mill to work in a grooming and boarding kennel. At first doing kennel work was just another way of earning a few extra dollars. A single parent with two children to raise, she worked two or more jobs on an ongoing basis, including waxing autos, construction work, and all kinds of hard manual labor, in addition to working the second shift at the carpet mill.

Lynn got her first break when the regular kennel helper left to work in an emergency veterinary clinic and Lynn became the full-time kennel help.

"What I really wanted," said Lynn, "was to have one job with reasonable hours and a comfortable income. I felt I owed that to myself and my children. Anyone who works in a mill knows that working hard for six months takes you as far as you are going to go. Everyone with the same job makes the same money. Seniority means nothing. With this thought in mind I decided I'd rather be part-owner of a kennel. Not wanting to give up the security of my small savings account I suggested to my boss that we establish a system whereby I could work my way into the business.

"Like everyone else in the kennel business she had trouble finding people who were interested in working in the kennel for long periods of time. My offer was ten years of work in return for 20 percent of the business—which computes to 2 percent per year. We agreed, with the stipulation that if I terminated my employment before the end of ten years I would get nothing. At the end of ten years, whether I stayed or not, I would get 20 percent vested interest or 20 percent of the current value of the kennel. It would be up to me to ensure that the value of the kennel increased by promoting good will and boosting business.

"The next thing that happened was the kennel manager who was also the head groomer graduated from college and went to work in a hospital caring for people instead of dogs. I was promoted and given her job. Also, my employer who was pleased with the way the incentive program was working for me, added a 50 cent bonus per dog visit to my hourly wage rate. By now I was putting in 30 to 40 hours a week at the kennel and still working at the mill.

"Several people, including me, suggested to the owner that she add a pet supply business to her operation. She had neither the time nor inclination to bother with sales, tax reports, ordering supplies, etc. But she did give me an opportunity to visit a trade convention in Miami at her expense so I could see what types of merchandise were available. On the way home I decided that merchandising was what I really wanted.

"I started with $500 worth of stock in one corner of the reception area. I had barely started when our groomer quit. I had been learning to groom and so I asked for the job, left the mill and went to work as a full-time kennel manager/groomer.

"My new contract gave me a weekly salary, five percent of the gross, a week's paid vacation, accident and health insurance and disability benefits.

"The following year I received a salary increase and an additional week's vacation (without pay), plus sick leave. That became two weeks' paid vacation and one week's paid sick leave, with the two percent per year agreement also still in force.

"I now have a pet store at the kennel and additional concessions in two other grooming shops in the area. My employer also pays half the fees for my continuing education in the kennel industry. I have taken a marketing and management course at a local college and completed the KenTech program offered by the ABKA.

"I am proud to be part of the kennel industry. My bonus percentage makes me work hard at increasing business at both ends of the operation, and my employer is happy to be free to do what she wants to do."

To me this represents an excellent example of two individuals working together for their mutual benefit. However, a certain flexibility is a must. So is the willingness to pay for services rendered.

The system that worked for Lynn Kittle would not work for everyone. Needless to say no agreement of this kind should be undertaken without the benefit of a legal contract. As time passes the memory dims, ideas change and so do circumstances. Put all long-term agreements in writing. Partnerships are like marriages, some endure better than others. Once relationships cool, good friends may find themselves in an antagonistic situation. That is part of human nature, the same as buying on impulse.

108

17

Kennel Computers

COMPUTERS CAN BE USED to make private and commercial kennels and veterinary hospitals more efficient in many ways: keeping track of inventory, monitoring business trends, calculating expenses, projecting profits, estimating taxes, keeping business records, computing the payroll, writing letters, keeping mailing lists current and even reminding you of important appointments. Kennel software is becoming more sophisticated all the time.

Programs for Kennels

There are programs available to record breedings, print pedigrees, update show records and more. There are also record-keeping packages designed especially for veterinary hospitals that help keep paperwork to a minimum.

Anyone engaged in the pet-care industry or operating a large hobby kennel should seriously consider the sizable benefits of computerization. As the country becomes more computer literate it will be almost impossible to function without one.

Essential Information

Individuals without previous computer experience should not be intimidated by these machines or the prospects of having to master a new skill, even in later life. Look on it as a challenge.

Most software is fast becoming user-friendly, with built-in instructions. If you can read you can use it—and you don't have to be a skilled typist by any means.

Selecting the right computer for your needs deserves careful deliberation. There is a lot of hardware (computers) and software (the programs they operate) available. One significant consideration is the availability of prompt repair service in case the computer malfunctions. Computers can be temperamental at times.

The basic requirements include a typewriter-like keyboard, a central processing unit with at least 256K memory, a single or double disk drive and a monitor. You may also want a near letter-quality printer and a modem.

A modem is the telecommunications link that, when tapped into the telephone lines, opens up unlimited areas of communication with the outside computer world and may be used to link together two or more computers in different locations. A printer is required for letter writing and other regular correspondence.

For some businesses leasing a computer system may be better than buying. It is possible to lease units with the option to buy later. Talk to your local dealer about the details.

The computer industry is still very volatile and the attrition rate is high. Companies are going in and out of business all the time, so shop around carefully and beware of so-called bargains; once a computer becomes obsolete it immediately goes on sale. I suggest buying all your hardware from an established company you know will be there tomorrow. While I have no special preferences, I bought my AT&T computer from a Sears Business Systems Center where I always receive prompt, helpful service.

This chapter was originally intended to be a comprehensive treatise on available hardware and software packages, but the industry is in such a state of flux that whatever I write today will probably become obsolete before this book is published. I would recommend what is known as IBM-compatible hardware: AT&T, IT&T, IBM, and a variety of others that handle IBM and IBM-compatible programs.

The amount of software available for IBM compatibles is almost unlimited, but not all programs are as easy to master as others. The IBM "Assistant" series is not as sophisticated as some but is relatively simple to use. Specialized kennel software is slowly becoming more refined and should be selected according to one's individual needs or preferences.

18

Bad Checks Can Be "Made Good"

AMONG THOSE WHO make a habit of it, writing bad checks is sometimes referred to as "making paper." There are so many people making paper these days that paying by check has become a major project. As a business person you are a potential victim, if you are stuck with a check that bounces. You do have legal options available for recovering the amount of the fraudulent check, which after all represents money you worked for and to which you are legally and morally entitled.

When a Check Bounces

If a bank returns a check due to insufficient funds, the payee usually redeposits it, hoping that it will have been covered. If a bank delays returning a bad check until after midnight of the next business day following the day on which the worthless check was received, by law the bank can be held responsible for making good the payment. The bank that misses its midnight deadline becomes accountable to the payee for the face value of the check. However, banks work overtime to insure that that does not happen.

If the check is for services rendered and for less than $100, don't bother going to the police. They are rarely interested and will usually advise you to consult a lawyer.

Protecting Yourself

There are a number of things that you should do to safeguard against becoming a victim. Number one is to require positive identification. Number two, be sure that the check carries the key items of information needed to contact the person writing the check in the event of insufficient funds.

Under normal conditions you should not accept a check that does not have the name of the branch, town and state where the bank is located. Be extra cautious with out-of-town checks and even more so with those from another state. If you are in an area where bank guarantee cards are used, ask to see a valid bank card.

Be equally cautious with checks that have not been personalized, imprinted with the customer's name and address, and those with low serial numbers. It is an established fact that checks numbered below 300 are more apt to bounce than those with higher serial numbers.

Think twice about accepting a check from anyone who seems nervous, drunk, wants to postdate the check or tries to rush you while you're checking identification.

One frequently used diversion is to pick up a small item, as if on impulse, and pay cash for it with a great deal of sorting through nickles and dimes, usually spread all over the counter. Don't allow yourself to be distracted. Always write the person's name, address and telephone number on the back of the check, along with some other traceable identification, such as the person's driver's license number. As most automobile operator's licenses now include the holder's photo, it's one of your best means of valid identification.

When It Happens to You

Here is a suggested procedure for handling bad checks that usually produces better than average results:

1. If a check is returned because of insufficient funds, call the issuing bank and ask whether or not the check is good for the specified amount. This is important. Honest bookkeeping errors can result in embarrassment for both the customer and kennel operator alike. If the check is good, redeposit it without mentioning it to the customer. Never redeposit a check without checking first to establish that it has been covered; never deposit one more than twice.

2. If the first step does not work, or the account has been closed, try to contact the individual by telephone.

    There is no need to be rude, but be firm. ("Hello, this is so-and-so from the kennel. Your check for X number of dollars was returned by the bank. I think it would be nice if you would come in and make it good.")

3. If the customer does not come in within two or three days, contact him or her again. If he is not answering the phone or the number is no longer in service, you must then send a registered letter asking the customer to call you or come in and settle the bill. The law requires that you either write or call and demand payment.

4. Go to Small Claims Court and file a claim. There is a short form to complete; a clerk will help you if necessary. A court date will then be assigned, usually at your convenience, as early as the court schedule will allow. The fee for filing is about $2.00. As procedures vary slightly from one community to another, you can obtain all the relevant information by contacting your local courthouse.

5. The defendant must then be served with a subpoena, a mandate requiring that person to appear in court at the specified date and time under penalty of law. You can either do this yourself or pay to have a marshal do it for you. If the server is a uniformed marshal it makes it look much more official and most people get pretty shook up about it. The next thing that usually happens is that they turn up on your doorstep very willing to make good.

   If you're not sure about the person's current address, especially if he or she has moved in the meantime, you can go to the post office and obtain the forwarding address for payment of a $1.00 fee.

When the customer comes to pay the bill, tack on any expenses that you have incurred during the collection process.

While collection may take a little time and effort on your part, it will give you some satisfaction to know that something can be done about those would-be tricky customers—regardless of whether the money or the principle is more important to you.

Although paying for your work time or merchandise with a bad check is tantamount to stealing, legally it is only classified as a misdemeanor. A misdemeanor carries a lighter penalty than a theft since a check may be collectible through civil procedures.

While you should talk with a lawyer about collecting on bad checks through the courts, in some jurisdictions you cannot collect through the criminal courts, period. The rationale is that you still have the account and no injury was suffered through the issuance of the check (depending on your point of view) since the account may be collectible through the usual civil action used for collection purposes. For the amount of money involved in grooming or boarding dogs it's hardly worth the time and aggravation of going to court.

In some states the writer of a bad check has a given number of days to make the check good after being notified by registered mail that you intend to prosecute. In a few states passing a bad check is punishable by a fine of up to $50.00.

Legally, you are not obliged to take anyone's check. Even if the person presents satisfactory identification the option is still yours.

Never discriminate when refusing a check. Don't tell a customer that you can't accept a check because he is a college student or lives in a bad neighborhood, etc. If you do so, you may be in violation of state or federal laws on discrimination.

This information is included only as an insight to possible options and may not apply everywhere. For legal advice talk to an attorney. In most areas there is a lawyer referral service operated by the county bar association which is listed in the Yellow Pages under "Lawyer Referral Service." The cost of the initial consultation is minimal and certainly worth keeping in mind before you become involved in any form of litigation.

Incidentally, if for any reason a customer should stop payment on a check as the result of a dispute, don't panic. Few people realize that a stop-payment order is good only for 30 days unless renewed. In most cases if you redeposit the check after the 30 days the bank will pay. Check with the bank if you have any doubts about the situation.

Please note: The Fair Debt Collection Practices Act prohibits threats, harassment and other abusive practices by so-called "third-party" bill collectors. A bill collector who violates the Act may be sued for damages by the creditor.

For more small claims court information, read *You Can Win Big in Small Claims Court* by James Norris. Over 1.5 million cases were heard in small claims courts last year.

19

Infectious Diseases

ALTHOUGH IT IS INAPPROPRIATE for kennel owners to play doctor, unless they choose to do so with their own dogs, it is essential that they know of the potential danger presented by the most common infectious diseases with which they will be confronted.

Despite widespread concern over the recent outbreaks of parvovirus, more dogs still die from canine distemper than from all other major diseases combined.

Canine Distemper

Distemper symptoms start six to nine days after susceptible individuals come into contact with the disease. High fever, bloody diarrhea, dehydration, runny nose and eyes, coughing, gagging, sneezing, lethargy, loss of appetite and respiratory distress are all indicative of distemper.

The prognosis varies with the individual; puppy losses are usually high. Hardpad, a disease characterized by hardening of the pads, may occur in tandem with distemper as a serious secondary complication.

Hardpad

Hardpad is attributed to a potent virus that attacks the weakened central nervous system, producing encephalitis, convulsions, violent muscle spasms and chewing fits. Survivors may develop chronic chorea (involuntary twitching and irregular muscle movements) and/or other prolonged side effects. Symptoms occur within six to nine days. Mortality is high.

A major outbreak of distemper and hardpad is a sobering experience and not soon forgotten. My first experience was with a litter of young adult Greyhounds in the late 1940s. Fortunately we saved all nine dogs, using a now antiquated treatment that apparently worked.

During the early 1960s, while managing a large Great Dane kennel, I experienced a vaccine breakdown affecting some 30 puppies and young adults. Working 24 hours a day we saved approximately 50 percent. It was a lesson in utter frustration.

With the improved vaccines available today, there is no valid reason to expose unprotected dogs to such debilitating diseases.

Infectious Hepatitis

Hepatitis invades most areas of the body, especially the liver. The severity of the symptoms varies. Extreme cases can induce total or partial paralysis. Indications include anemia, tonsillitis, excessive bleeding, loss of appetite, runny eyes, listlessness, fluctuating fever, trembling, vomiting, excessive thirst and abdominal distress.

The virus is transmitted in the urine of infected carriers; incubation takes from six to nine days. This disease may also occur in conjunction with distemper. It is estimated that a high percentage of all dogs contracting hepatitis recover spontaneously without exhibiting outward clinical symptoms.

Leptospirosis

Leptospirosis is commonly contracted from bacteria in the urine of infected dogs or rats. The onset of symptoms is rapid: lack of appetite, weakness, fluctuating temperature, reluctance to stand, frequent urination, bloody diarrhea, bleeding gums and complete debilitation. Mortality is high, especially in puppies.

Parvovirus

Parvovirus made a worldwide impact in the late 1970s and early 1980s, since which time vaccines have been developed to reduce its drastic effect on the world's canine population.

The onset of parvo is frequently indicated by vomiting, diarrhea, fever and other signs that the dog is not feeling up to par. Infected dogs may not exhibit obvious symptoms, and sometimes it is difficult for veterinarians to make an accurate diagnosis. As vaccine breakdown has been reported, parvo symptoms should receive medical priority.

116

Coronavirus

Corona mimics parvo in many ways. The most common symptoms are gagging and regurgitating yellow bile, and passing smelly, mucous-coated stools. The onset of symptoms often occurs within 24 hours of exposure. Treated promptly, symptoms subside just as quickly as they appear. A coronavirus vaccine is being developed and is expected shortly.

As both parvo and corona viruses can survive for extended periods in favorable environments, it is important that kennel operators keep their facilities sanitized and disinfected in order to minimize cross-infection. Medical researchers have recommended using a 2 percent solution of Clorox® bleach to control parvo and corona virus in kennels and runs. However, the manufacturers issued a statement saying that they made no such claims for their product, and actually have a warning on the label clearly stating that the product is hazardous to humans and domestic animals.

My yard was apparently contaminated after a dog brought the disease home from a dog show. So far, each dog I brought home since that time has contracted the disease to some degree. I have used a variety of products in an attempt to destroy the virus with no noticeable success.

Rabies

Rabies, an infectious disease that can affect all mammals, is most frequently transmitted in the saliva of an infected animal as a result of a scratch or bite. Prolonged exposure to rabid animals has also been cited as another less frequent mode of transmission.

Rabies symptoms mimic those of lesser diseases and are not always clearly identifiable, even by experts. During the 1950s one human rabies case in the Chicago area was wrongly diagnosed as polio. Two of my associates treated a dog for gunshot wounds for a week, including force-feeding it, before it went into convulsions and was diagnosed as rabid. Both underwent the Pasteur treatment and suffered no lasting harm from their experience.

Although incidents of rabies in domestic animals have increased over the past few years, the situation is not considered critical. Even so, it has been estimated that as many as one million head of cattle may die annually in this country as a result of bat-induced rabies.

Human Diploid Cell Vaccine (HDCV) has now replaced the long-standing Pasteur treatment as the preferred method of aborting rabies; HDCV is not as painful and requires fewer treatments to be effective.

Canine Cough (Tracheobronchitis)

Canine cough has plagued kennel operators for many years. This highly contagious throat and bronchial infection is typified by a dry, hacking cough, which may induce retching and gagging to relieve catarrhal irritation in the respiratory tract. Although canine cough rarely lasts more than two or three weeks and is not life threatening, it does create owner anxiety and is bad for business. The dog's apparent distress soon disappears once it returns home. Fortunately there is now a vaccine available to help control this annoying affliction.

Brucellosis

An infected carrier bitch can spread brucellosis through vaginal discharge or by being bred. An infected bitch is most contagious after whelping or having an abortion. The disease, also called Malta or Mediterranean fever, also affects goats, hogs and cattle and is transmitted in their milk. All breeding stock should be tested prior to mating as a safeguard.

Examining New Arrivals

While there is no guarantee that a dog incubating a serious disease will never enter your kennel, regardless of precautions, it is a sound policy to keep the odds in your favor by being careful.

All new arrivals should be carefully screened to insure they are not displaying obvious symptoms of sickness. No attempt should be made by unqualified persons to diagnose specific ailments, but the animal's apparent health and state of well-being should be noted and recorded in its file for future reference.

Start at the head. Check the eyes for signs of distress, pain, inflammation, discharge, ulceration or other unusual problems. Make sure the nose is not running, or dry, or cracked. Check the mouth for abnormal odor, bad teeth, bleeding gums or abnormalities of the tongue or mucus membrane.

Check the ears for discharge, odor, inflammation, excessive hair, or tenderness when handled. Look behind the ears for fleas, ticks or irritation caused by scratching.

Run your hands over the dog's body, feeling for ticks or foreign objects buried in the skin—especially with long-coated breeds.

Check the genital and anal area. Lift the tail and look for dried tapeworm segments around the anus. Establish if females are in heat. If so, ask the owner when the heat started. If possible, have the owner lift the dog up onto its back legs so you can examine its belly and in between its hind legs for signs of fleas. If the area is red and irritated that usually means fleas, even if none are visible. Another indication would be black flecks stuck to the skin, representing flea droppings.

Whenever you discover anything that seems unusual, tell the owner and record it in the dog's file.

20

Controlling Pests
and Parasites

A KENNEL OWNER is forced to deal with a formidable assortment of pests and parasites on a continuous basis. Ticks, fleas, flies and mosquitoes top the list, followed by ants, mice, rats and roaches. Ticks are the most durable, flies the most plentiful, fleas the most annoying, mosquitoes the most irritating, ants the most persistent, mice the most destructive and rats the most alarming. Roaches are probably the most anonymous.

Flies

Flies are just about everywhere. Although not as plentiful in arid desert regions during the heat of the summer as in more humid regions, flies are rarely in short supply. In some states, like Florida, it is necessary to have runs screened in to protect dogs from flies and mosquitoes. It is hard to decide which of the two is more dangerous to unprotected animals.

Flies will eat away a dog's ears before you realize something's wrong. They become particularly tenacious once they draw blood. Ticks-Off® is an effective fly repellent, stronger than Flys-Off®, and can be used to prevent the problem from getting out of hand. Another frightening aspect of persistent fly problems is the possibility that they will lay eggs on the dogs, which will then hatch into larvae and burrow under the dog's skin and do serious, sometimes fatal tissue damage.

I found that electrical bug-zappers kill flies, but in doing so attract every curious flying insect in the neighborhood—many of them too smart to get zapped. Alternatives are fly bait, pest strips, stink traps or frequent fogging.

Located far enough away, stink traps work well; I prefer them to excessive spraying or fogging, which I consider unhealthy to pets and people alike.

A partial solution is to keep the environment as free from waste and garbage as possible to avoid attracting flies to the area in the first place.

Dogs exposed to flies should be examined regularly.

Mosquitoes

Mosquitoes are carriers of heartworm; they infect dogs while engorging themselves. Mosquitoes breed in all kinds of unlikely places where there is enough stagnant water for their eggs to hatch. Old containers, empty cans and especially old tires all make convenient hatcheries for the pesky mosquitoes.

Salt-marsh mosquitoes are the most dangerous, and the biggest. While I lived in Delaware heartworm was a major concern until preventive medication became available. For the boarding kennel owner it is important to insure that boarders requiring heartworm medication receive it as prescribed. One person should be solely responsible for dispensing medication so that there is no mix-up.

Fleas

Fleas are equally partial to most warm-blooded mammals. These flat-sided, wingless insects are intermediate hosts for tapeworms, and in parts of the desert Southwest are responsible for the reemergence of bubonic plague, the black death of the Middle Ages in Europe.

Less common at high elevations and where humidity is low, fleas are common in most areas of the United States. Where climate conditions are favorable, fleas are a serious problem because of apparent immunity to most pesticides.

Fleas develop in four stages: egg, larva, pupa and adult. The females need a blood meal before laying their eggs—which they do both on their host and in its habitat. This meal may come from any convenient host including dogs, cats, humans or any other animal.

Adult fleas live on the host while feeding. The female starts depositing her eggs two or three days following her first meal and continues to do so for several weeks, producing up to 1,200 eggs.

The eggs hatch into larvae within a few days; larvae can be fully developed in a few weeks. However, under unfavorable conditions, they may take several months to mature, spin their cocoons and make the transformation to pupae, which, depending on conditions, will grow into adults in as little as a week or take up to a year to complete its life cycle. Adult fleas survive without food for 12 months and it may require drastic measures to rid a badly infested facility of these pests. For areas where parasites are a major concern there are now built-in automatic spray systems available. I have no experience with such innovations and the merits of installing such a system should be reviewed in detail on an individual basis.

The ideal conditions for flea propagation include proper temperature and humidity and available hosts. In hot, arid climates their life expectancy is relatively short. Semitropical conditions are a Mecca for fleas.

According to veterinary dermatologists, flea bite allergy accounts for approximately 80 percent of the pruritic (itching) dermatitis seen in dogs. This common skin problem is induced by hypersensitivity to an irritating substance in the flea's saliva. The result may be itching and scratching—resulting in self-mutilation and outbreaks of moist eczema, frequently referred to as "summer hot spots."

The eradication of fleas on dogs and cats must be done in conjunction with treatment of the premises, where the parasite's life cycle begins. Such a program must include the use of a product with residual effects, such as ones containing 5 percent carbaryl, which acts as a stomach poison on flea larvae and a contact poison on adults. Synergized pyrethrins provide instant knock-down power. When reinfection is probable, repeated treatment is usually necessary. For infestations in the home, fogging or professional pest extermination may be the best solution.

Ticks

Ticks are almost indestructible. It has been estimated that if the world were exposed to enough radiation to kill every living creature, ticks could still survive for several years. Not a pretty thought.

Ticks are anywhere and everywhere but seem to prefer dense wooded areas and heat to cold. On the East Coast, oldtimers say that ticks arrive with the lilac. I found that to be reasonably accurate.

Both male and female ticks must feed before they breed. Soon after mating the male leaves the host and dies. The female, after engorging with blood, drops off the dog and seeks a suitable spot to deposit the 4,000 to 6,000 eggs she will lay during the next two weeks to one month. After she has deposited her eggs she also dies.

The egg incubation period ranges from 27 to 57 days, at which time tiny larvae or seed ticks emerge. In order to become a nymph, which is the next stage of development, seed ticks must feed for four to five days—usually on mice or other rodents. When fully engorged the seed tick leaves its host and finds a suitable place where it can develop into a nymph. After feeding for six days on an available host, usually a small mammal, the nymph abandons its host and molts for the final time. In warm climates the entire molt may take three to four weeks. In colder areas the tick may winter in one of its developing stages and finish the cycle in spring.

After molting, the nymph is an adult and ready to repeat the cycle once again. Ticks that as larvae feed on one animal, as nymphs on another and as adults yet another are referred to as three-host ticks. Included among these are the American dog tick and the Rocky Mountain wood tick. Both are carriers of Rocky Mountain spotted fever, which is most prevalent in the eastern part of the country. About 1,000 people contract the disease annually.

A newly emerging tick-borne disease called babesiosis has spread south from Cape Cod and Martha's Vineyard to Long Island, New York. The primary victims are campers, and as many campers take their dogs with them kennel owners in the Northeast are potentially at risk. The disease was first identified in 1926. Symptoms include muscle pain, fatigue, fever, anemia and an enlarged spleen. Individuals whose spleen has been removed are at serious risk. Under microscopic examination the disease is said to resemble malaria.

The normal treatment for curing tick-infested animals is to dip them with one of the many pesticides available for that purpose. Thoroughly read the label instructions before you start. This is doubly important when switching from one brand to another. Don't assume that any two products are alike. Be doubly careful if using dips and flea and tick collars. There are an estimated 70,000 different pesticides being manufactured in this country. Some are chemically incompatible with others and combining two or more of these could be dangerous.

Kennel operators in many areas of the country have made tick dipping mandatory for all incoming boarders as a safeguard for all concerned. There is a lot to be said for that; however, special precautions should be taken if the dog or cat has been wearing a flea collar. The active ingredients in certain collars and dips may not be chemically compatible and if combined may induce toxic reaction.

The San Diego Regional Poison Center is one of several that have expressed concern over the increase in the number of pet poisonings believed to be associated with indiscriminate use of flea and tick pesticides. Overused, these products can be ingested by licking or absorbed through the skin in potentially dangerous quantities.

Inhaling spray mist or chemical vapor is also dangerous. When dipping several dogs it is advisable to wear protective clothing and a mask. The use of rubber gloves is especially important in preventing the absorption of toxic amounts of chemicals into your system through the pours of your skin. Rinse all containers, including the tub, launder the towels and wash your hands thoroughly with soap when you're done.

A limited number of products are made with no toxic chemicals or petroleum distillates, making it safe to use on puppies and young adults sensitive to conventional pesticides.

Different poisons produce a variety of symptoms when toxic reaction is taking place, including: drooling, trembling, abdominal pain, rapid or shallow breathing, vomiting, convulsions, depression, coma and possible death. Any indication of unfavorable reaction should prompt an immediate call to your veterinarian. If unable to contact a veterinarian, call your local poison control center or one of the following numbers:

New York City (212) 340-4495; Chicago (312) 942-5969, (312) 292-5391, (312) 978-2000; Ft. Worth (817) 336-5521, Ext. 17, at night (817) 336-5527; Los Angeles (213) 669-2401.

As poison hotlines are being established nationwide, it seems like a good idea to have the local number prominently posted by each telephone.

Cockroaches

Cockroaches, apart from being undesirable pests, have been linked with the spread of toxoplasmosis in humans via a complex food-chain process originating with infected cat feces and going from cat to cockroach to bird or mouse and back to cat. Simple contact with infected cats can transmit the disease to humans. The cockroach itself can also contaminate human food with infectious toxoplasma oocytes—as can flies..

While there are an unlimited supply of pesticides available, I have always favored using the services of a professional exterminator to keep pests under control.

Rats and Mice

Rodents are notorious for their ability to spread disease. Because most poisonous products used to kill rats and mice are potentially dangerous to dogs and cats, I have always preferred traps to poison bait. The trick is knowing how to set the traps effectively. Cheese is not the bait mice like best. Chocolate or butter is more tempting. Sprinkle a small amount of the bait you are using on the floor around the trap as a taster. After each kill, wash the trap thoroughly to remove the "death" smell, or it will act as a warning to the next potential victim. Change the locations of the traps slightly every day. If this system doesn't work, put a cat on your payroll. Not all cats are suited to being kennel cats, however, so choose carefully.

Rodents thrive where there is an abundant food source, especially if allowed to propagate undisturbed. Find and destroy all possible rat and mouse habitats. Keep food in protective containers.

If you live in a rural area, harvest time and the onset of cold weather bring rodents indoors. Be ready for them.

Internal Parasites

Internal parasite problems are of more concern to hobby kennel owners than boarding kennel operators. Although care must be taken to prevent boarders from infecting each other, there is no effective way to screen newcomers without a stool check.

The four principal types of worms to be concerned about are roundworms, tapeworms, hookworms and whipworms. Internal parasites can infest both young and old dogs during any period of their lives.

There is widespread belief that worms can be detected in dog stools. This is partly correct. Roundworms and tapeworm segments are sometimes passed and visible in the stool. However, the absence of visible evidence does not preclude the possibility of an infection. The only reliable method of diagnosing internal parasites is with a microscopic examination of the stools. The exception is the tapeworm, which is usually identified by finding dried segments attached to the hair around the anal area.

Hookworms and whipworms, which attach themselves to the stomach lining, are rarely passed and even more rarely seen with the naked eye. Whipworms are about two inches long and shaped like a whip. One-third of its length represents the body, while the remaining two-thirds is the thread-like tail. Hookworms are little more than one-half inch long and resemble an exaggerated letter "C."

While there are plenty of all-purpose worming remedies on the market, the most effective treatment is to isolate the specific parasite species and use the appropriate anthelmintic for each separate variety.

Types of Parasites and Parasitism

Commensalism—a partnership of two different organisms which benefits one and neither benefits nor harms the other.

Ectoparasite—lives on the skin of the host, such as a tick, flea or louse.

Endoparasite—lives inside the body of its animal host.

Obligate Parasitism—needs a host to exist.

Parasitism—a parasite in partnership with another organism, where one lives at the expense of the other.

Pathogenic Parasite—does harm by injecting an injurious substance into the body of its host.

Kennel Sanitation

Puppies kept in dirty, unsanitary surroundings are prime candidates for numerous health problems associated with both internal and external parasites. The solution is obvious enough. Any dog suspected of being infected by parasites should be isolated and treated before coming into contact with other dogs in the kennel.

Controlling pests and parasites requires determination and persistence, and cannot be approached casually. The best we can expect to do is keep the situation under control.

While under normal circumstances one need not be concerned about personal health problems associated with handling domestic animals, cross-infections can occur and good sanitation practices are essential whether operating a hobby or business operation.

Cats are social animals. Once they are neutered most males and females will coexist peacefully with one another. Because of the risk presented by highly contagious feline diseases like pneumonitis, rhinotracheitis and feline infectious anemia, the desirability of communal confinement in a boarding situation is debatable.

21

Mange and Other
Skin Disorders

THE TERM "MANGE" has too often been used to describe just about every type of skin disorder imaginable, many of which might more accurately be described as nonspecific dermatosis. Mange is actually the specific name of a limited form of skin infestation by tiny parasites known as mites. The type of mange is determined by the type of mites involved; the two main types are sarcoptic and demodectic. Diagnosis is not easy to make, even by an experienced professional. If you suspect a dog may have mange, advise the owner to consult a veterinarian.

Mange may occur during any season of the year. The sarcoptic form of mange is highly contagious and spreads rapidly from one dog to another. Special care should be taken after handling a dog that has a suspicious-looking skin condition. All equipment coming into contact with the animal must be sanitized for the protection of other clients' dogs and your own reputation.

Types of Mange

Demodectic mange, also known as demodicosis, red mange or follicular mange, is caused by *demodex folliculorum,* a mite present in small numbers in about 85 percent of all healthy dogs. Only about 1 percent eventually develop clinical symptoms of the disease. In such cases mites suddenly multiply and invade the skin tissue in large numbers, resulting in skin irritation and loss of hair.

126

Demodectic mange is often attributed to stress. It may suddenly appear following injury, pregnancy or illness. Although it occurs in older dogs, puppies three to 12 months of age are most frequently affected. Dobermans, Pit Bull Terriers and Dachshunds are predisposed to infection but no breed is totally immune.

Localized demodectic mange may first appear as small balding spots and red, irritated skin around the eyes, nose, lips and sometimes front legs. The affected area is not usually itchy. The hair loss may spread into a generalized demodectic mange, which is one of the more severe skin ailments found in dogs. The infected areas become encrusted and infected with bacteria and large pustules may develop all over the body, resulting in redness, swelling and itching.

Treatment may take the form of both injections and topical medication. Antibiotics are needed to help control generalized infection. Severely infected animals may take months to recover and some never recover completely.

It is generally agreed that demodectic mange is not contagious from dog to dog or from dog to man.

Sarcoptic mange, also known as scabies, is caused by a mite called *sarcopes scabiei*. Unlike demodectic mange, this disease is highly contagious to other dogs and can also be transmitted to human beings. The first indications may be small swellings with bloody crusts on any part of the body. The edges of the ears and the elbows are frequently affected. Because of intense itching, dogs with scabies usually scratch violently, causing sores and subsequent skin infections.

Positive diagnosis depends on both clinical signs and a microscopic examination of skin scrapings to identify the mite. Treatment includes injections and medication to relieve the itching and medicated dips to destroy the mites. In bad cases it may be necessary to clip the dog to the skin. Once the generalized infection is under control, local areas can be treated more effectively. Even so, complete recovery may take two months or more.

Ear mites, or ear mange, is caused by *otodectes cynotis*, a mite that lives only on the surface of the skin, spending most of its life in the area of the outer ear. While it is most common in cats and rabbits, it is also found in dogs. It is highly contagious.

Symptoms of ear mange include constant ear scratching and head shaking. It is not unusual for animals to make the back of their ears raw by continually scratching or to develop ear hematomas from shaking their heads. Diagnosis is made by positively identifying the mite using magnification.

Ear mange is not difficult to cure with medication. Treatment may have to be repeated over the period of two or three weeks. If the problem recurs it is likely that the animal is being exposed to reinfection.

Skin Disorders

Collie nose, a particularly unattractive form of dermatitis, is almost exclusively confined to Collies, Shetland Sheepdogs and "farm collies" but it has also been observed in Boxers, Cockers and retrievers. It is attributed to an allergic reaction to the sun. The only certain cure for this condition is to keep the animal out of direct sunlight. The use of PABA sunscreening lotion and / or PABA tablets sometimes helps, as does tattooing the nose to compensate for lack of pigmentation. Collie nose should not be confused with mange and is not contagious.

The problem of unsightly skin disease in dogs may be more than just skin deep. Disorders in the dog's blood and immune system can play a role in mange and other chronic skin diseases, say veterinary scientists.

In dogs with skin disease, certain blood cells may not be as responsive as they should be. These cells, called lymphocytes, should help fight and protect against infections. Nonresponsive cells mean the dog's immunity is lowered, making dogs with skin disease heal slowly and susceptible to other infections. The cells do not respond normally because something in the blood suppresses the cells; these suppressors keep the lymphocytes from combating the disease and infection.

Bacterial skin infections, which often accompany and complicate mange, cause the suppressors to appear and affect the cells, scientists have found. The problem of suppressors hampering the cells disappears if the bacterial infection is cured. Originally, mites were thought to be linked to the unresponsiveness of white blood cells.

Further study is being made to identify what the suppressors are and how they make cells unresponsive. The mysterious suppressors aren't the cause of skin disease, but they do hamper the immune system's ability to fight skin disease caused by infections.

Skin diseases are a common health problem in dogs and cause concern for owners and kennel operators alike. As extended medical treatment for skin ailments is frequently unsuccessful, it pays to be alert to early warning signs of possible skin disease to avoid the possibility of contaminating other dogs in the kennel, in the event of a contagious condition.

Skin problems have also been traced to poor diets. One report alleged that skin ailments in eleven dogs were traced to what was termed "generic dry dog food." Rapid improvement was said to occur after changing these dogs to a nationally known brand of dog food that met with all NRC nutrition requirements.

22

Allergies to Dogs and Cats

ALLERGIES TO DOGS and cats are similar to other common allergies, such as those due to plant pollens and mold spores. Allergies are acquired by inhaling various types of organic materials that the body reacts to. In susceptible people, inhaling organic substances like plant pollen causes the release of an antibody (called *reaginic* or IgE antibody) in response to the presence of that particular substance.

An individual with a specific IgE antibody is said to have an allergy to the offending substance. When the allergic person makes contact with that substance, he or she will have a predictable reaction, which we recognize as allergic symptoms: sneezing, runny nose and itchy eyes (hay fever), or coughing, wheezing and shortness of breath (asthma). An individual may be allergic to one or many different agents.

Allergic symptoms vary in intensity from one person to another depending upon how much IgE antibody they produce and how much of the causative agent they inhale. Allergies to offending substances may come and go, but frequently last for years. Prolonged exposure to causative agents will continually aggravate chronic allergic conditions.

It is estimated by medical researchers that upwards of 20 percent of the U.S. population is afflicted with one type of allergy or another. The National Institute of Allergy and Infectious Diseases has been studying the problem of allergies at home and in the work place to learn more about this widespread affliction.

Many people become allergic to all kinds of animals, including dogs and cats. The substance that causes the allergy is generally found on the animal's skin, particularly in the dander, or scales, normally shed from the outer layer of skin (the epidermis). It is not part of the hair, as often erroneously supposed, although it may be found attached to the hair. The same agent is also found in animals' blood, saliva and sometimes urine.

Individuals working around animals—kennel help, groomers, veterinarians, laboratory workers, ranchers, etc.—may develop allergic reactions to a wide variety of danders. A former veterinarian from Kingman, Arizona, had to abandon his practice after 16 years because he developed breathing difficulties as a result of allergies to animals. He became a chiropractor.

The late Mary Johnson, a Great Dane breeder, was allergic to her dogs and had to take shots so that she could pursue her hobby; her famous Marydane kennels produced many winners over the years. Obviously, for Mary, the sacrifice was worth making.

The final diagnosis of allergy disease should be made by an allergist and confirmed by administering skin tests for reactions to different substances, including extracts of animal danders. In occupationally related cases, some allergists will recommend a series of allergy shots to desensitize the sufferer. This form of therapy has been reported effective enough to reduce symptoms sufficiently to allow individuals to continue working with animals. However, the treatment may be required on a continuing basis and not everyone feels that dedicated to working with animals.

Individuals who are known to be allergic to pollens and other reactive agents run the most risk of becoming allergic to dogs and cats and probably should not become kennel workers or groomers.

Allergies to animals sometimes develop only after prolonged exposure. Minimizing the amount of airborne particles of dander in the air by controlling the air circulation and using hepa filtration equipment will help reduce the risk of developing allergies to the animals you are working with.

Because of the substantial number of individuals involved, allergists have adopted a more constructive approach to pet-induced allergies. In the past the stock answer to this problem was to advise people to dispose of their pets, or stop working with animals. In the light of ongoing research, allergies to animals may someday become a thing of the past. In the meantime, those of us who are afflicted with this irritating condition will have to survive as best we can.

I'm not altogether sure that it is worth mentioning, but it has been reported in medical journals that some individuals are allergic only to one breed of dog or cat. The evidence supporting these claims is not overwhelming but, reportedly, in certain cases symptoms appeared only when patients were exposed to Siamese and not Persians, or Collies and not Poodles, and so on. Why this happens is not known.

130

23

Diseases Communicable from Dog to Man

I HAD REASON to visit a tuberculosis sanitarium on numerous occasions. At that time tuberculosis was not as under control as it is today and the prospect of being exposed to this highly infectious and dangerous disease was very unsettling. Everyone entering the hospital wards, which reeked of powerful disinfectants, was required to wear a gauze mask for protection. You soon got the feeling that airborne bacilli were swarming all over you like ants at a picnic. I daresay it was not uncommon for first-time visitors, overcome by a feeling of impending doom, to try to hold their breath during the entire length of their stay. I know I did. Seasoned visitors seemed to derive sadistic delight in watching newcomers squirming apprehensively every time a patient went into a coughing spasm.

Somehow, despite the initial trauma, after several visits people seemed to relax, talking and laughing as unconcerned as if in their own living room. The danger was still as real as ever. What made the difference? Familiarity. Why? Because familiarity breeds contempt. When we are overexposed to any given situation we tend to become blasé. Sometimes, too blasé.

The Need for Caution

For that same reason, almost everyone who handles dogs for a living gives little or no consideration to the fact that dogs are capable of

131

transmitting over 60 communicable diseases or infections to man. Cat lovers may like to know that there are 39 diseases that can be transmitted from cat to man.

Here's a test. How many of the following diseases are directly transmittable from dog to man?

anthrax	mumps
amoebic dysentery	rabies
brucellosis	ringworm
bubonic plague	Rocky Mountain spotted fever
chicken pox	roundworms
coronavirus	scarlet fever
diptheria	strongylosis
heartworm	salmonella
hemorrhagic septicemia	toxoplasmosis
hookworm	trichinosis
leptospirosis	tapeworm
measles	tuberculosis

The answer: All these and more.

Anthrax, brucellosis, diptheria, leptospirosis, mumps, measles, ringworm, scarlet fever and tuberculosis can be contracted by coming into close contact with an infected dog.

Hemorrhagic septicemia (harmful bacteria living and growing in the bloodstream) and rabies result from bites from infected animals. The recommended procedure following a bite is to wash the wound with plenty of soap and running water for between 15 to 20 minutes in order to reduce the risk of possible infection. Rabies is on the upswing, especially among cats. Vaccination of both dogs and cats is being urged by many health departments.

Amoebic dysentery and salmonella come from ingesting contaminated food.

Hookworm, strongylosis and toxoplasmosis can be contracted when parasites are absorbed through broken skin and can affect the bloodstream, internal organs and subcutaneous tissue.

Roundworms are contracted as a result of swallowing roundworm eggs; tapeworm by swallowing an infected flea. Trichinosis, although communicable from dog to man, is usually contracted by eating insufficiently cooked pork. Swine is the most frequently infected domestic species.

Rocky Mountain spotted fever usually results from a bite from an infected tick, but crushing one against the skin may also cause infection. Over 1,000 cases are reported in the United States annually. Ticks should never be handled with bare hands. The incubation period for spotted fever in man varies from two to 12 days. The actual onset may be preceded by a

132

loss of appetite, listlessness and headache. The usually sudden onset is marked by chills and high fever. Sometimes nosebleed may occur. Fever reaches its peak during the second week and is expected to run its course in about three weeks. The disease is characterized by a rash, usually on the wrists and ankles, spreading to the back, arms, legs and finally to the stomach. Sometimes the palms, soles, face and scalp are also affected. Fatalities in untreated cases run to about 20 percent.

Bubonic plague is contracted from a bite by an infected flea, or by being bitten or scratched by an infected animal. Cuddling her plague-infected cat proved fatal or one Nevada woman, while a girl in Oregon was hospitalized but survived after breaking up a cat fight. Bubonic plague is most prevalent in the Four Corners area of the desert Southwest. Health officials blame flea-infested rodents for the problem.

Neither roundworm nor hookworm are well-suited to a human host but in their larval state will invade the subcutaneous tissue causing subcutaneous abscesses. At times they will bore tunnels under the skin usually affecting the head, trunk and forearms, a condition known as "larva migrans" or creeping eruptions. Larval filaria may also migrate to areas of the body, such as the eye, brain and liver, where they can create serious damage to sensitive tissue.

Tapeworm in humans is quite a common problem; however, I view the supposed practice of seeding tapeworms in a person's stomach in order to induce weight loss as some kind of brain sickness. Tapeworm-induced cysts up to two inches in size have been removed from people's lungs or liver, sometimes after many years of painful discomfort.

Few well-informed pet-care professionals are aware that diphtheria, measles, mumps, scarlet fever and tuberculosis are transmissible from dog to man. This is particularly significant to kennel workers because some people, especially children, like to have the company of their pets when they are confined to their sickbed. Fortunately, most of us have had our shots or are otherwise immune to most of these diseases by virtue of previous contact, usually during childhood; otherwise this could be a real problem.

Updated studies indicate that up to 25 percent of all family dogs have been affected by canine coronavirus. Incubation for this disease is one to three days. In humans it induces a variety of flu-like symptoms, including upset stomach, headache, diarrhea, nausea, lethargy and sore throat. Recovery time varies according to treatment, after which one is presumed to be immune from further infection.

Ask yourself these questions: Do I wash my hands every time I handle a dog or cat, especially before it has been washed? For smokers, do I put my cigarette down on the grooming table then back into my mouth? Ugh! We've all heard someone say that dogs are cleaner than people. That's an arbitrary statement, to say the least. Dogs are disinclined to watch where they are stepping, and mine certainly are not allowed to put their feet up on the table. Have you seen owners dancing with a dog? You know, holding its front feet while the dog walks on its hind legs. How about eating some "finger food" directly afterwards without taking time to wash one's hands? It is not a smart practice.

The complete list of diseases communicable from dog to man is mainly comprised of scientifically named disorders that have little or no meaning for most people.

Many of these communicable diseases occur very infrequently; however, some have as high as a 95 percent mortality rate. While chances of contracting some of these ailments are remote, a certain element of risk is present for those who handle animals for a living.

I know of three dog groomers who contracted diseases from dogs, four counting myself. One person told me that she suffered for more than a year before being cured. I contracted coronavirus.

It is possible to work on an infected animal without realizing it. For example, an article in the *Journal of the American Animal Hospital Association* titled "Rabies Can Be Insidious" discussed the case of a Poodle brought to the Animal Neurological Clinic in Richardson, Texas, after being struck by a car. The dog was in shock, essentially unable to move, with blood and contusions (bruising) about the head. Brain decompression (removal of excess pressure on the brain due to increased fluid) was attempted but the dog died ten days later. During the interval the dog was conscious most of the time. Vision apparently was lost and there was overreaction to external stimuli, head pressing and constant pacing— symptoms attributable to the effects of the head injury. However, the autopsy revealed unexpected histopathological findings: rabies. Diagnosis was confirmed by pathologists at Texas A & M University and the Communicable Disease Center in Atlanta, Georgia.

It was later learned that two dead bats had been found in the dog owner's yard, one of which tested positive for rabies. In the meantime 22 people were exposed to the case, all of whom were advised to undergo rabies vaccine treatment.

Canine brucellosis is another disease communicable to man and the subject of considerable research by a leading pharmaceutical company, which developed a new diagnostic test that is expected to pick up many previously undetected cases that might present a threat to humans making contact with these infected dogs. Unlike cattle-induced brucellosis, which is contracted by drinking raw milk and known as undulant fever or Malta fever, researchers are still uncertain exactly how canine brucellosis is transmitted to humans.

Compounding the problem of diagnosis for doctors is that symptoms in man—fever, chills, headache and a feeling of being unwell—mimic those associated with many other types of illness. In the past, some cases have been misdiagnosed as mononucleosis (an infectious disease characterized by sore throat and swollen glands). When patients didn't respond to treatment, a check of pets with which they had been in frequent contact often revealed canine brucellosis. Patients recovered after a course of special antibiotic treatment.

"We don't suspect canine-induced brucellosis to be widespread," said Dr. P.R. Glick, marketing vice-president for Pittman-Moore, Inc. and a veterinarian himself. "We are reasonably certain, however, that many dogs have the disease right now, imperiling other dogs and humans. Undoubtedly people are going to their family physicians complaining of the disease symptoms, but physicians are still too unfamiliar with the disease to consider it a possible cause."

As a precaution it would seem a good idea for dog owners to have their pets tested for brucellosis. The disease affects a dog's reproductive organs in particular. In the male, abnormal sperm or an inability to mate are common symptoms. In an infected female, the abortion or early death of fetal puppies often occurs. Any unexplained reproductive failures in either male or female dogs could be indicative of brucellosis. Dogs should be tested before breeding.

Meliodosis is a disease with a 95 percent fatality rate among humans that can be transmitted via the dog. The first cases contracted in the United States were recorded in 1951. Victims suffer acute or subacute septicemia (bacteria living and growing in the bloodstream), which causes death. Chronic forms may last for months or years. Apparently the infection is not passed directly from person to person. Just how the infection occurs remains uncertain, but it is believed to be the result of an insect bite. Either the flea or the mosquito may be responsible for transmitting the disease.

Leptospirosis is an infectious disease that can affect all mammals— including man. It is usually transmitted through bacteria in the urine and absorbed into the system through cuts, scrapes or sensitive tissue. The disease also passes under the names Weil's Disease, mud fever, trench fever, swineherd's disease, rice-field fever, spirochaetal jaundice, Japanese autumnal fever, Japanese seven-day fever, Canicola fever and flood fever.

The number of incidents of leptospirosis among humans is much higher than generally supposed. Symptoms include fever, chills, depression, weakness, weight loss and rash. Many areas of the body are affected but it mainly infects the kidneys. Most cases are described as being "relatively mild" and frequently go undetected or are diagnosed as being one of the more common bacterial or viral diseases. Of particular significance to women, leptospirosis is frequently responsible for fetal death and abortion.

Animals, especially dogs, may continue to be carriers of leptospirosis for a considerable period following recovery from the disease.

In addition to a large number of diseases, dogs may also harbor some

20 parasites communicable to man or vice versa. Possibly the greatest source of potential danger are animals that come from a pound or animal shelter, or puppies from facilities where sanitary conditions are less than ideal.

When handling dogs in the course of our daily work, we should pay particular attention to the common sense rules of good hygiene. Keep all cuts and scrapes protected from possible infections. Wash your hands with soap and water after handling animals. Sanitize your tools, tables, floors, cages, etc. Watch what you put into your mouth—that includes cigarettes, candies or any other edibles you may handle prior to washing your hands.

The purpose of the foregoing remarks is to alert kennel workers to the fact that there is a certain amount of real danger associated with the profession that should not be taken lightly. Sanitary working conditions are essential to everyone's continued good health.

All kennel employees should be encouraged to wear protective dust masks, especially when brushing, combing or cleaning up after dirty animals, as a preventive measure against inhaling potentially harmful particles that may contaminate the air they breathe.

An Actual Case History

After writing an article for *Petcare Professional Magazine,* I received the following letter from a dog and cat groomer describing a recent experience with a cat-transmitted disease, toxoplasmosis.

I am writing you today to share a nightmarish experience which has consumed me totally over the past year. It is my intent to spare other pet groomers the possibility of contracting toxoplasmosis, a disease generally spread by cat feces.

Earlier this year, I became ill with what I assumed was flu. When my symptoms failed to go away after a few weeks, I decided to have a talk with my doctor. Preliminary tests showed nothing. From there I went to an internist, who proceeded to give me a thorough physical and more tests. Still I had no answers to why I was running a low-grade fever, having peculiar abdominal pains, backaches and a general feeling of fatigue.

The situation went from bad to worse and in September I was forced to give up my grooming job; I just did not have the energy to carry on. Meanwhile, my doctor continued to run tests trying to determine why I was sick. It was only recently after he ran a series of tests for what he called "exotic diseases" that a diagnosis was finally made. Toxoplasmosis is difficult to diagnose and takes a special blood test to determine its presence.

The past year has cost me dearly in time off work and medical expenses. I think it would be worthwhile for you to devote some space in your magazine to this disease.

I am sure that nowadays many pet groomers handle cats, and they should be made aware of the danger of contracting this disease. My doctor has told me I may return to work as this disease is "self-limiting." I am now on my way to recovery. I was advised to wash my hands and arms thoroughly after handling each cat.

Toxoplasmosis is a serious infectious disease caused by the protozoan *Toxoplasma gondii* (a disease-causing, one-celled parasite found in a number of animals, including those used for food). While the disease may be either congenital or acquired, infection is generally attributed to contamination by cat feces. Toxoplasmosis is most prevalent in southern and tropical regions, and least prevalent in northern regions and in Rocky Mountain areas.

It is estimated that one child in every 1,000 to 2,000 is born with congenital toxoplasmosis, causing eye and brain damage. Although studies can determine whether the disease is being transmitted by the mother through the placenta, prenatal treatment is difficult because the necessary drugs may harm the developing fetus. Less effective drugs have to be given to prevent undesirable side effects.

Toxoplasma protozoans can be introduced into the body either through improperly cooked meat, by coming into contact with infected soil, or through exposure to contamination by cat feces. The latter is deemed the most probable.

The time it takes for the disease to develop after exposure to the pathogen varies and even in known cases tests will often prove negative during the early stages. The first areas affected are the lymph nodes, resulting in painful swallowing and tenderness.

The protozoan multiplies rapidly, spreading throughout the body. The severity of the disease will depend on:
1. The strength of the patient
2. The strain of Toxoplasma
3. The degree of infection

During the final stages of the disease symptoms are quite similar in both the acquired and the congenital variety: skin rash, lung congestion, fever and enlargement of the spleen are indications of toxoplasmosis. Yet, since these symptoms mimic those of numerous other ailments, diagnosis is not an easy task, and definitive answers require extensive laboratory tests. Treatment with antiparasitic drugs is usually successful but symptoms can recur.

In addition to the preceding letter, another person wrote telling about having a tapeworm-induced cyst surgically removed from her lung. This condition was apparently the result of inhaling either a tapeworm segment or tapeworm eggs many years before and was diagnosed following X-rays to determine the extent of a rib injury. Initially, cancer was suspected.

While not overly common and certainly no cause for undue alarm, these incidents clearly illustrate the need to observe sensible precautions if handling a high volume of dogs, cats or other animals on a continuing basis over an extended period.

If you suffer from prolonged or unusual symptoms that fail to respond to traditional treatment, consult with your doctor about the need for more extensive diagnostic tests to either confirm or preclude the existence of so-called exotic diseases.

24

The Public's Attitude
Toward Animals

AMERICANS LOVE THEIR PETS. This fact makes the pet-care industry an unusually secure business venture when approached correctly. Here is some interesting information concerning the type of individuals kennel proprietors can expect to deal with.

Survey Findings

According to a survey of over 3,000 adult Americans made by Dr. Stephen Kellert of Yale University, owning pets was surpassed only by watching animals on TV as the respondents' most frequent pet-related activity. During the two years prior to the interview, 78 percent had watched a TV wildlife show, 67 percent owned a pet and 46 percent had paid a visit to the zoo. Despite this apparently high level of interest, the survey seemed to indicate that most Americans know relatively little about animals in general and wildlife in particular. Fifty-eight percent indicated that they felt more concerned about the suffering of individual animals than about endangered species or animal population levels in general.

There was noticeable regional differences in knowledge and attitude concerning animals. Alaskans were the most knowledgeable, followed by those in the Rocky Mountain states. Northeasterners were least informed. Pacific Coast residents seemed more concerned with animals' rights. Those in the southern states were more concerned with the animals' practical or material worth.

There are an estimated 35 million dogs and as many cats in the United States. The increase in the pet population has been viewed with alarm by both humane organizations and conservationists, who are calling for the control of pet reproduction to reduce the large number of animals being destroyed annually in animal shelters. One estimate put that figure at over 13 million annually.

Most experts believe that the biggest obstacle to controlling the pet population is the attitude of the dog-owning public. A survey of 500 California dog owners revealed that the majority of those who did not plan to have their pets neutered were concerned that the surgery might affect their pets' personality or appearance. Moreover, 63 percent of those who planned to have their females spayed expressed a desire to have at least one litter prior to the operation. Most owners were under the erroneous impression that having a litter before being spayed would make the bitch a better pet. Other reasons given were that a friend or relative "just had to have" one of the puppies, or that the kids wanted her to have puppies. Pure-bred dog owners expressed a desire to recoup part or all of their initial investment. Experience will teach them otherwise, no doubt!

Benefits of Companion Animals

At an International Conference on the Animal/Companion Bond, sponsored by the Center for the Interaction for Animals and Society and the University of Pennsylvania, it was established that an important role is played by companion animals in our society, especially among the elderly, the handicapped, and autistic children. Animals can and do make significant contributions to the continued good health of their owners.

Pets help us unwind. It has been demonstrated that one's blood pressure drops while watching fish or petting animals.

A startling revelation from a study made by British social workers over several years revealed that in many instances abused pets led to homes with abused children. This tends to accentuate the need for continued humane education. A previous study indicated that, in the majority of cases, individuals convicted of brutal or violent crimes, mass murders, rape, etc., as children displayed a marked tendency toward animal abuse. However, these social issues have little to do with kennel business.

A three-year study on the American public's attitudes and behaviors toward animals was commissioned by the Fish and Wildlife Service of the U.S. Department of Interior. This two-part investigation identified nine basic attitudes toward animals, together with their intercorrelation and approximate frequency of occurrence in the American population and the distribution of these attitudes among various social, demographic and animal-activity groups.

Attitudes Defined

The nine basic attitudes toward animals were labeled as naturalistic, ecologistic, humanistic, moralistic, scientistic, aesthetic, utilitarian, dominionistic, and negativistic attitudes. The attitude concepts, broadly defined as distinguishable patterns of related ideas, feelings, and beliefs, were defined as follows.

The Naturalistic Attitude. The naturalistic attitude is associated with an interest in all animals, but specifically demonstrates a profound attraction to wildlife and to the so-called "great outdoors." The naturalistically oriented have affectionate feelings for pets but tend to regard them as inferior to wild animals. A primary satisfaction comes from direct personal contact with the wilderness, and wildlife is particularly valued for the opportunities it provides for activity in the natural environment. An occasional manifestation of this attitude is a deep feeling of inner satisfaction experienced when using the wilderness to escape the daily pressures and setbacks of modern man's existence.

The Utilitarian Attitude. The main characteristic of the utilitarian attitude is the perception of animals in terms of their practical or profitable qualities—their material benefit to humans. The utilitarian attitude is not necessarily marked by a lack of affection for or interest in animals, although such feelings are usually secondary to the more predominant concern in the usefulness of animals. While many utilitarian-oriented persons own pets, most believe they should be trained for specific tasks and not kept only as companions or friends. Persons with a utilitarian attitude tend to be indifferent to issues of animal welfare that do not affect the animal's performance or practical value.

The Dominionistic Attitude. A sense of superiority and a desire to master animals are identifying characteristics of the dominionistic attitude. Animals are usually regarded from the perspective of providing opportunities for dominance and control, and expressions of ability and skill in competition with animals are typically emphasized. Considerable attachment to animals may accompany the dominionistic attitude, but usually in the context of obedience training competition and rodeo events.

The Negativistic Attitude. A number of distinctive attitudes are included within the negativistic category, the common feature being the desire to avoid animals. Typical of the negativistic attitude are feelings of indifference, dislike, fear and superstition. This viewpoint is marked by a fundamental sense of separation and alienation from the natural world. For many negativistically oriented persons, a gulf in emotion and spirit separates animals from humans. The negativistic attitude is clearly people-oriented, allowing little if any sense of empathy or kinship with animals.

The Ecologistic Attitude. The ecologistic attitude is primarily oriented toward wildlife and natural settings but typically is more intellectual and detached. This attitude views the natural environment

140

predominantly as a system of interdependent parts. Rather than focusing on individual animals, wild or domesticated, the major emphasis and affection is for animals in their natural habitats. Accompanied by considerable knowledge of animals, this interest tends to concentrate more on behavioral relations of animal species than on their physical or biological properties.

While adhering to the notion that man is just another animal species, and ultimately as dependent on the natural environment as any other, the ecologistic attitude tends to be concerned with protecting the environment for all humankind. Associated with this view is an interest in modifying modern society's impact on the natural world by compromising between practical human requirements and protection of natural habitats.

The Humanistic Attitude. The humanistic attitude is distinguished by strong personal affection for individual animals, typically pets more than wildlife. The pet animal is viewed as a friend, companion and member of the family. The love of the humanistically oriented person for animals can rightly be compared to that felt for human beings. Although not specifically interested in wildlife, humanistically oriented people often extend their empathy for pet animals to a general concern for the well-being of all animals, including wildlife. This concern for animal welfare is not associated with ethical philosophy or in any particular concern for animal species and is more an extension of feelings being extended from pets to wildlife.

The Moralistic Attitude. The most striking feature of the moralistic attitude is a great concern for the welfare of both wild and domesticated animals. Rather than deriving from a strong affection for individual animals (as in the humanistic attitude) or from consideration for animal species (as in the ecologistic attitude), the moralistic attitude is typically more philosophical and based on ethical principles opposing the exploitation and the infliction of harm, suffering or death on animals. The moralistically oriented person objects to activities involving the killing of animals—hunting, trapping, etc. They also oppose the exploitation of animals in rodeos, cage zoos, horse and dog racing and tend to perceive a kinship or sense of equality between humans and animals.

The Scientistic Attitude. The scientistic point of view is characterized by an objective, intellectualized, somewhat circumscribed perspective. Animals are regarded as physical subjects for study, not as objects of affection or moral concern. There is little personal attraction to pets, wildlife or the natural environment among the scientistically oriented. Animals are usually perceived as the means for acquiring specific knowledge (mainly physiological, biological and taxonomic) or as offering opportunities for problem-solving. The affective relationship is one of emotional detachment, with curiosity often constituting the primary motivation for interest in animals.

The Aesthetic Attitude. The aesthetic attitude also tends to be associated with emotional detachment, but with a central interest in the beauty of symbolic properties of animals. Although many people possess a feeling for the physical attractions of animals, the aesthetically oriented base their interest almost exclusively on this artistic appeal. The aesthetically oriented tend to be attracted to animal sporting activities involving considerable artistic display, such as animal showmanship, fox hunting and bullfighting. For the most part they remain aloof from the living animal, enjoying it more as an object of beauty (in paintings, sculpture, movies) or of symbolic significance (in poetry, children's stories, cartoons).

These nine attitudes should be regarded more as conceptual impressions of general human tendencies than as specific human behaviors. Most people generally possess more than one attitude, feeling and behaving a certain way in one situation but changing attitudes under other circumstances. Also, while individuals may express a certain attitude, rarely do they exhibit every characteristic of this attitude. In other words, not only do people demonstrate multiple attitudes, they also vary considerably in the intensity of their commitments in general. However, in most individuals it is possible to identify predominant characteristics of a primary attitude toward animals.

Related to the expression of multiple but hierarchical attitudes in individuals is the question of which attitudes tend to cluster with one another.

The relative popularity of the attitudes can be examined in terms of both their prevalence (total number of cases in the population) and their incidence (rate of new cases within a given time period). Prevalence figures provide a good idea of absolute frequency, while incidence figures suggest historical changes and trends. Tentative prevalence statistics from the national study suggest that among Americans the humanistic, utilitarian, and the indifference component of the negativistic attitude top the list. Then comes the scientistic, aesthetic and ecologistic. Considering incidence over a ten-year period, the impression is that the utilitarian attitude is decreasing in popularity along with the negativistic, while the naturalistic, humanistic and ecologistic viewpoints appear to be substantially increasing. National study data comparing different age, educational and urban-rural groups generally corroborate this change.

The report on the distribution of attitudes in the general American population indicates that middle-aged women are more concerned with protecting animals from suffering and are much more inclined to express strong loving feelings toward their pets. Men were found to be more utilitarian and expressed a greater acceptance of such activities as killing animals for meat, predator control and hunting. Farmers and ranchers were the most utilitarian group, expressing the belief that animals exist largely for the benefit of man.

Being a kennel operator obviously requires you to interrelate with many different types of individuals. It is good to know that an owner's viewpoint on animals and animal care may not always coincide with your own. I believe that experienced kennel personnel will have little difficulty identifying individuals from the nine groups categorized in this chapter.

25

Your Nose Knows

TO EMIT ODOR a substance must first produce a gaseous vapor. Our sense of smell is governed by the yellow to brown colored olfactory cells that line the inside of the nasal cavity and cover the sieve-like membrane over the sinuses. The ends of the olfactory cells are covered with fine, sensitive hair called cilia. Our ability to detect odor is dependent on that gaseous vapor becoming trapped in the olfactory portion of the nasal cavity. As few as 40 odor molecules are enough for odor detection.

The way that our olfactory mechanism works is still a mystery. The nerve impulse, set in motion when the odor molecules make contact with the cilia, travels through the olfactory system to that part of the brain that controls our sense of smell and makes us aware of the presence of odor (this is considered the most primitive portion of the brain, probably due to the fact that as man became civilized his sense of smell became less and less important to his survival: locating food, sensing danger, finding a mate; the percentage of man's brain devoted to odor detection is proportionately far smaller than that of any other animal).

Strangely enough the odor perception center of the human brain is close to and interrelated with the centers for both memory and emotions. This would tend to explain our reactions to certain odors. For example, a particular fragrance or odor can recall an incident or event to mind with remarkable clarity, while a scent subconsciously associated with an unhappy experience may produce a negative response without our knowing the reason for it.

Response to a particular odor can depend upon the circumstances. For example, while the aroma of roast beef is usually regarded as a pleasant one, a certain wild flower that emits a similar odor is generally considered nauseating.

Some odors, like vanilla, can easily be detected in parts per billion in air. The sense of odor being ten thousand times more sensitive than that of taste, much of the so-called food "taste" is really odor perception. That is why food may not taste as good if you happen to have a cold or a stuffy nose.

Our olfactory sense is basically lazy and in the presence of a powerful odor may cease to function effectively in as little as two or three minutes. This is why those constantly exposed to objectionable odors soon become oblivious to them. Workers in kennels or grooming shops are frequently unaware that there is an odor problem that their customers may find disturbing. For that reason it is important for us to take positive steps to control odor. The most common methods now being used are:

1. Temporarily inhibiting the ability to smell by using a strong chemical to destroy the sense of smell.
2. Masking an objectionable odor so that it cannot be detected. Some masking agents have a sweet odor that may sometimes prove to be as offensive as the one it is masking.
3. Using ultraviolet radiation, especially when incorporated into a central air circulating system, as an effective form of odor control.

A more recent odor control concept that may prove effective was recently developed. It involves increasing the molecular weight of odor so that it cannot form a gas. No gas, no odor. This complicated chemical process produces a totally odor free environment for both kennel workers and customers alike.

Free odor control information is available from Dualle Products (957 Huron Dr., Elgin, IL 60120), a pioneer company in the manufacture and distribution of safe dog and cat odor-control chemicals.

26

What Makes
Good Kennel Help?

THE PERPETUAL PROBLEM confronting boarding kennel owners is the lack of competent, conscientious staff. A good kennel worker embodies a number of basic qualities rarely found in combination: intelligence, keen observation, inexhaustible patience, understanding of animals, orderliness, an inborn aptitude for handling a pooper-scooper and the capacity for hard work.

The need for intelligence is frequently overlooked on the assumption that you don't need a high I.Q. to take care of a few dogs and cats. While that is essentially true, the individual must have sufficient intelligence to understand the importance of specific instructions when dealing with animals that require special or restricted diets, or some type of medication. Couple intelligence with keen observation and you reduce the risk of sick or ailing dogs going unnoticed. Coughing, sneezing, watery eyes, runny nose, diarrhea, loss of appetite, etc., may or may not be indicative of disease. However, such symptoms should never be overlooked. The slightest indication that an individual is off-color should be noted and the animal checked, preferably by a veterinarian.

Patience and understanding are the two virtues most frequently lacking in kennel help whose prime motivation is earning a living. The majority of kennel employees are probably overworked and underpaid by today's standards. Unless they really love their work they soon become disenchanted—sometimes venting their dissatisfaction by abusing the hapless animals in their charge.

Finally, many individuals, no matter how much they love animals, may find daily kennel chores repulsive. Add shift work, sometimes seven days a week during the busy season, and it's a miracle we can get help at all.

In the final instance it is the kennel operator who is always on standby. When someone is sick, needs the day off or whatever, the owner or manager must fill in, regardless of his or her personal situation.

The composite of the ideal kennel aide is an extremely intelligent, highly observant and industrious animal lover who is never sick, always punctual and works mainly for the love of animals and is not concerned with the money involved. If you find one or more of these rare individuals you are more fortunate than most.

The single most important quality for a good employee, and one that is getting progressively harder to find, is honesty. Inside theft costs American businessmen an estimated $40 billion annually. Robberies account for only 10 percent of the $50 billion in unaccounted-for losses, or shrinkage as it's known. (That is 2 percent of the gross national annual retail sales, estimated at $2.5 trillion.) Vendor theft takes 15 percent; employee error, damaged inventory and other factors take 30 percent; shoplifting accounts for 5 percent; and employee theft of cash and goods makes up the balance of the remaining 40 percent. That means the people we employ and trust bilk us for over $20 million annually. That reflects sadly on the state of our society. Most workers apparently feel entitled to all the fringe benefits they can get their hands on. Whatever happened to honesty and integrity?

When the kennel building faces in the right direction, block dividers can be an asset in the amount of shade they create as the sun moves from east to west. These runs will not be in full sun until late in the day.

In this kennel the need for shade has been addressed by topping the runs with aluminum sheeting. Some owners use only a single width of sheeting at the gate-end of the runs. In addition to providing shade, sheeting also serves as an effective escape-proof barrier.

148

27

How Safe Is Your Kennel?

J UST HOW SAFE is my operation? I wonder how many kennel owners have ever even thought to consider that question? The fact that you have never had an accident is no insurance against having one in the future.

There are several areas of potential danger in every kennel. Safety is something that should concern us all, without being paranoid about it.

While most areas may be comparatively safe, there are usually one or two that could use a second look. Here are some of the areas where problems might occur.

Electrical Circuits

Does your electrical wiring system comply with the latest national and local electrical code? Electricity is something that most of us have come to take for granted. Yet it can be dangerous if not under control. Aluminum wiring installed during the 1960s and early 1970s is known to be dangerous and should be checked by an electrician and modified accordingly.

In some cases the electrical outlets are a mass of "temporary" adaptors and extension cords. This highly dangerous practice should be avoided as much as possible. If you need additional outlets, have them professionally installed. If fuses are continually blowing as a result of an overload, don't just beef up the fuses. Have the circuits checked and rewired as necessary. The same applies to circuit breakers.

Be certain that all appliances that need grounding *are* grounded. Never handle electrical appliances around the bathtub. It could result in a fatal shock whether switched on or not. Don't handle appliances when your hands are wet.

Cages

Are your cages constructed well enough that even the most persistent or pesky animal is both safe and secure? If bars are too wide apart there is always a possibility that dogs may get their jaws trapped or that small puppies may get their heads trapped between the bars. If cages are constructed of a diamond-shaped wire mesh it is possible for most breeds to get their toes or pads trapped in it.

When you use cage dryers, be sure that there is enough ventilation around the back and sides so that dogs will not be overcome by heat or lack of oxygen; this is especially important with older animals or those that are difficult to handle. Most fiberglass cages are poorly ventilated. Dogs have died while being dried in this fashion.

If you have to leave dogs unattended while they are cage-drying, it is a good idea to have the dryer on an automatic timer or, alternatively, use only low heat. Rapid Electric makes an excellent timing device adaptable to all heavy-duty dryers.

Even when there is adequate ventilation, dogs will often jam themselves against the nozzle of the dryer, resulting in a bad skin burn. You can always explain to the owner that it was all the dog's fault, but somehow they're not buying that these days. High velocity dryers, using no heat, help avoid this.

Security

Could someone enter your establishment and remove a dog without your knowledge? All doors leading in or out of the premises should be equipped with warning bells or buzzers, and with automatic return springs so that doors cannot be inadvertently left open. There should be at least two closed doors between the dogs and the outside world.

Recently a dog escaping from a grooming room allegedly bit a customer on the way out. The unfortunate proprietor was sued for $50,000 damages. The escaped dog was never caught. Under certain circumstances a second lawsuit might also have been initiated. Luckily, it was not. As of writing this book, the initial litigation was still pending.

Self-Protection

The well-being of the kennel owner and the employees is also a matter for concern. Sometimes kennel workers are faced with the problem of protecting themselves from their customers. Unfortunately, there are

In sun-belt areas like Florida, California, Arizona, etc., heavy-duty nylon screening is frequently used. Using colorful scenes also brightens up the drab appearance of the kennel area.

Unshaded, uncovered runs like this one could pose serious legal problems in the event that a boarder escapes or dies from heat prostration.

Each of these runs is protected by two sliding sun screens that are fixed to the fence posts with standard tracks. This allows the screens to be adjusted and thereby provide maximum or minimum sun protection or exposure throughout the year.

151

always one or two owners who would jump at the opportunity of making easy money. We are all potentially vulnerable to a wide assortment of legal harassment. Several dog groomers have been threatened with law suits for various so-called wrongdoings, ranging from causing bodily injury or emotional trauma to putting dogs in the wrong clip—or, perhaps more correctly, for misunderstanding what the owner wanted.

It obviously pays to clarify all areas of doubt before accepting animals. For your grooming room, a complete set of grooming charts is indispensable. New customers should be required to indicate which type of clip they want so that groomers can be sure that when they say "Dutch" they mean Dutch and not Town and Country, or whatever.

General Conditions

In general are your working conditions conducive to a safe operation? Do you have a nonslip mat in your bathtub? Do you have steps up to the tub for the bigger dogs to use?

Keep the thermostat on your hot water heater below 140 degrees to avoid the risk of scalding dogs and cats during bathing.

Sterilize your equipment to eliminate the likelihood of cross-infection. Use tearless shampoos to minimize eye irritation. Do not use cosmetic products not formulated for dogs and/or cats that might cause allergic or toxic reactions. Never mix two chemicals, like different brands of flea and tick dip, together. Use aerosol sprays with care, especially around the eyes.

Keep all tools sharp and clean. Dull, rusty clipper blades and shears are a needless hazard. Use restrainers to discourage dogs from falling or jumping off the grooming table or out of the bathtub. Should a dog or cat jump off a table and injure itself, you may have to prove that you took reasonable precautions to prevent an accident. Never leave an animal on the table unattended.

Make sure your work areas are adequately illuminated. Poor light causes eye strain and that contributes to fatigue. Fatigue in turn reduces your power of concentration, making you susceptible to mistakes. Lighting fixtures need not be expensive or elaborate, but they must be located so that sufficient light goes where it is needed.

During the time when ticks and fleas are abundant and you must dip several dogs a day, wear rubber gloves so you will not become overexposed to potentially harmful chemicals. Always read the instructions on the label before using any new pesticide product.

As carriers of Rocky Mountain spotted fever, ticks represent a potential health hazard. Don't handle ticks with your bare hands; always use forceps when removing them from animals. If one attaches itself to you, don't panic. Dab it with rubbing alcohol and it will withdraw its head from under your skin—a important safeguard against possible infection.

152

For hobby kennels, self-waterers can be easily attached to any convenient water source.

The raised sleeping area is an interesting innovation. Most kennel owners expressed varying dissatisfaction with store-bought pallets or bed boards because, they said, dogs either destroyed them or used them as toilets. Note the self-waterer attached to the far wall.

This hobby unit combines individual runs and a partially shaded exercise paddock. Note the individual dog houses, which can be used as shelter from the elements. This is a daytime only facility; all the dogs are taken in at night.

One drain is usually sufficient to service both outside runs and inside pens.

153

Be alert for all contingencies during the course of a normal working day. Don't take anything for granted. Both dogs and cats have the instinctive ability to find any weak spot in your operation. There are always a handful of boarders who exhibit an inherent capacity for self-destruction. If you learn to identify these when they arrive you can save yourself a great deal of grief.

When you leave the building, be sure that all appliances are unplugged to help reduce the chances of an electrical short. Disaster is most likely to strike when no one is at home. One Christmas morning about 90 cats and dogs boarding at an animal hospital in Rhode Island died when a fire broke out while everyone was gone. Only one dog was saved. The cause of the fire was believed to be an electrical malfunction.

28

Law Suits Over Dogs

W HILE IT IS CONCEIVABLE that dog owners have been involved in disputes of one form or another since time began, one of the first recorded court cases involving *Canis familiaris* in this country dates to 1869.

Burden v. Hornsby (Old Drum), 1869

The civil action revolved around the shooting of a hunting dog, Old Drum, owned by the plaintiff, Charles Burden. It was alleged that the dog was shot and killed on the order of the defendant, Leonidas Hornsby.

Old Drum was found about a mile from Hornsby's farm, lying with his head in water, just above the ford on Big Creek. His body was riddled with buckshot. There were sorrel hairs on the body, suggesting that it had been carried some distance. Hornsby owned a sorrel mule. On the basis of this circumstantial evidence and the fact that Hornsby previously admitted he had told his nephew to shoot a stray dog, an act provoked by stray dogs killing a number of his sheep, Burden brought suit for damages before a Justice of the Peace at Kingsville in Johnson County, Missouri.

The first jury failed to agree, but in a second trial Burden won the verdict. Hornsby appealed to the Johnson County Court of Common Pleas at Warrensburg, requesting a retrial on the grounds of new evidence. Refusing to give up the case despite persistent threats and community unrest between those taking sides, Burden hired the law firm of John F.

Phillips and George Graham Vest, leading lawyers in that part of the country at the time.

Hornsby was represented by Thomas T. Crittenden, who later became governor of the state and was credited with dispersing the Jesse James gang.

George G. Vest, as always, was the most colorful figure in the courtroom. A graduate of Center College in Danville, Kentucky, at the time of the "Old Drum" trial Vest was 40 years old and one of the upcoming men in the state, an astute lawyer and accomplished speaker.

The trial was held on a rainy day in a dim, lamp-lit courthouse and included many witnesses for both sides. According to the *Kansas City Star*: "More oratory was turned loose than was ever heard in the most celebrated murder case ever tried in a Missouri court."

After indicating the weakness of the arguments of the opposing counsel and drawing the attention of the jury to the law applicable in the case, Vest delivered what has been described as the most moving testament to the abiding nature of a dog's love for his master:

> Gentlemen of the Jury: The best friend a man has in this world may turn against him and become his enemy. His son or daughter that he has reared with loving care may prove ungrateful. Those who are nearest and dearest to us, those whom we trust with our happiness and our good name may become traitors to their faith. The money that a man has he may lose. It flies away from him, perhaps when he needs it the most. A man's reputation may be sacrificed in a moment of ill-considered action. The people who are prone to fall on their knees to do us honor when success is with us may be the first to throw the stone of malice when failure settles its cloud upon our heads. The one absolutely unselfish friend that a man can have in this selfish world, the one that never deserts him and the one that never proves ungrateful or treacherous, is his dog.
>
> Gentlemen of the Jury, a man's dog stands by him in prosperity and in poverty, in health and in sickness. He will sleep on the cold ground where the wintry winds blow and the snow drives fiercely, if only he may be near his master's side. He will kiss the hand that has no food to offer, he will lick the wounds and sores that come in encounters with the roughness of the world. He guards the sleep of his pauper master as if he were a prince. When all other friends desert, he remains. When riches take wings and reputation falls to pieces, he is as constant in his love as the sun in its journey through the heavens. If fortune drives the master forth an outcast in the world, friendless and homeless, the faithful dog asks no higher privilege than that of accompanying him to guard against danger, to fight against his enemies. And when the last scene of all comes, and death takes the master in its embrace and his body is laid away in the cold ground, no matter if all other friends pursue their way, there by his graveside will the noble dog be found, his head between his paws, his eyes sad but open in alert watchfulness, faithful and true even to death.

156

The jury took only two minutes to bring in a verdict in favor of Burden, assessing damages of $50. For his unforgettable tribute to the virtue of all dogs in what has been described as the most celebrated dog case in the world, Vest received a fee of $10.

Since that time a bronze tablet has been attached to a wall by the old courthouse in Warrensburg, now the home of the Johnson County Historical Society, marking the scene as an historical site. Also, a monument stands on the back of the Big Creek just above the crossing where Old Drum was found shot. The memorial contains in its construction rocks sent from most American states, the Great Wall of China, the White Cliffs of Dover and many other countries. On the base is a bronze plaque bearing the legend of Old Drum. This noble monument was dedicated in 1953 by the attorney general of Missouri and the late Captain Will Judy, one of the most prolific dog writers of all time and the late owner/editor of *Dog World* magazine.

Caswell v. Swavola

"Poodle's Haircut May Cost Barber $15,000"; "Couple Sues Pet Spa, Claims Dog Scarred"; "Fearless Friend or Crazy Dog? Court to Decide." Those were some of the headlines in Florida newspapers during mid-1974. TV stations from home and abroad covered the story in graphic detail.

A law suit filed on behalf of Robert and Evelyn Caswell alleged that their Toy Poodle was changed from a fearless friend to a nervous wreck as the result of an injury sustained while being groomed by Frank Swavola in a National Pet Spas' mobile unit at the Caswell's beach home in Fort Lauderdale, Florida.

According to newspaper reports, the plaintiffs charged that their two-year-old Poodle was transformed from "a spry, alert, fearless member of the Caswell family" into a dog that was "cold and nervous." Also, because they believed that hair would never grow back over the wound, the owners feared they would never be able to show their AKC registered Toy Poodle.

According to Marie Swavola, the owner of National Pet Spas, the dog was obese and oversize. But the Caswells still asked for $5,000 in compensatory damages to help pay the dog's medical bills (the wound, about the size of a quarter, did not heal normally and required corrective surgery) and to compensate them for their mental anguish. An additional $10,000 in punitive damages was also requested.

National Pet Spas denied the allegations and counter-sued for $12,500 in damages for defamation of character and damage to its business reputation.

In addition to numerous unfavorable newspaper stories and national TV coverage of the incident, the owners of National Pet Spas alleged that the plaintiffs were harassing them and their customers to such an extent that customers were scared off by sheer intimidation and that their grooming business was being ruined. One example was a notice in the classified section of a local paper which read: "Large reward for info. Our female Poodle was severely and permanently injured by a door-to-door dog groomer. Anyone experiencing this type of incident please call. Family grieving. . . ."

As National Pet Spas operated the only mobile unit in the area, there was little doubt in anyone's mind who was implicated. Those not wishing to get involved in the squabble took their business elsewhere. So did those who subscribed to the theory that it's better to be safe than sorry.

According to Marie Swavola, her husband Frank admitted applying a caustic coagulant to an existing wound, about the size of a quarter, which he discovered while brushing out the dog prior to grooming. Frank insisted he did not cut the dog and suggested that the injury may have been caused by the Caswells' other dog, which apparently had a tendency to chew on the Poodle.

While the correlation was never fully explained, the Caswells also claimed that their beloved Toy Poodle required surgery to remove an ovarian cyst as a direct result of the grooming injury.

At a pretrial hearing, judge Stewart LaMotte ordered the dog to be examined by a veterinarian and the Caswells by a psychiatrist.

One newspaper quoted Mrs. Caswell as saying that she was "no animal nut" and that personal gain was not her purpose. "We want to expose these people so that they won't do this to someone else's dog," she is reported to have said.

Evidence was presented to the court along the following lines:

On Saturday, January 27, 1973 at 8:00 a.m. professional dog groomer Frank Swavola of National Pet Spas arrived at the home of the Robert Caswells and parked his mobile grooming van in the driveway, as he usually did. He then collected both Poodles owned by the plaintiffs. After the dogs were groomed, Swavola and an assistant returned them to their owners and left.

Later, Mrs. Caswell noticed that one of the dogs, called "Little One," had a cut on its flank close to one of its hind legs. The dog was taken to a veterinarian, who treated the injury. Additional treatment was given to the dog by the Caswell's regular veterinarian, who was not available when the wound was first discovered. Surgery was performed to remove the tissue damaged by the caustic coagulant, which inhibited proper healing.

The groomer did not mention the wound to the dog's owners, and during the trial stated that the cut was there prior to the dog being groomed. He admitted that he applied the coagulant to stop the cut from bleeding.

On the second day of the trial, which was held in June 1974, Little One was brought into court. Everyone was curious to see the dog's reaction, since Mrs. Caswell had stated that the Poodle was like a "retarded child and unresponsive to the attention of her loved ones." She also claimed that the dog had become afraid of bearded men. Frank Swavola had a beard. However, the dog approached him with no apparent show of fear, according to an eyewitness report.

Early in the trial, a psychiatrist appointed by the court testified that he found no evidence of any lasting effects of the alleged "mental and emotional pain suffered in anguish" by the plaintiffs attributable to their dog's condition. Still, the jury awarded the Caswells $1,500 in compensatory damages and $7,500 in punitive damages, for a total of $9,000.

The judgment was appealed by the defendant and, according to the owner of National Pet Spas, the case was settled out of court for the amount of the Caswells' legal fees.

The reason for the out-of-court settlement had something to do with the alleged discovery that the plaintiff had a past history of suing for large sums of money at the least provocation; this fact might have impeached the credibility of their testimony claiming no interest in personal gain.

The case reportedly cost National Pet Spas over $5,000 in legal fees. The unfavorable publicity ruined the business.

Other Legal Actions and Opinions

A lawyer friend of mine was involved in a law suit resulting from a German Shepherd bitch disappearing while being boarded. Not a particularly good example of the breed, she had produced one litter of ten healthy puppies.

The owner claimed he had sold her puppies for an average of $150 each—or $1,500 for the litter. By his calculations this bitch was therefore capable of producing 20 pups annually for the next ten years. On that basis, he assessed the dog's worth at $30,000 as a brood bitch. He asked an additional $20,000 in punitive damages.

The trial lasted two days, during which time several expert witnesses were called by both sides to testify regarding the quality of the bitch, her potential as a brood bitch and the possibility that she might produce valuable champion offspring.

At the end of the two days, after hearing extensive testimony from both sides, the judge called the opposing lawyers to the bench and said: "I'm not interested in all this nonsense. What I want to know is if this dog was shut up in a cave and allowed to have puppies naturally, what would they be worth?"

Armed with the answer to that profound question, he awarded the plaintiff $750 in damages.

By the time he paid his attorney, the bitch's owner had little to show for his trouble. The defendant, despite what might be considered a relatively small judgment, was compelled to invest many times that amount in legal fees and the cost of providing expert witnesses to testify on his behalf.

Legal Precedents

Unfortunately, most of the precedents being used to prove negligence in cases relating to animal injury or loss date back many years and most involve veterinarians. Here are a few examples of such opinions:

"The veterinarian is under no legal duty to treat any animal" (Lathan v. Elrod, 6 Ala. App. 60 So. 428—1912). "Nevertheless, once he has accepted the duty of treatment, whether gratuitously or for hire, he becomes liable for any negligence and cannot abandon his obligation without reasonable notice to or prior agreement with the animal owner" (Boom v. Reed, 69 Hun. 426, 23 NY Supp. 421-Sup. Ct. 3d Dept.—1893).

"The duty of care begins when the veterinarian [kennel proprietor or groomer] first approaches the animal" (McNew v. Decatur Animal Hosp., Inc., 85 Ga. App. 54, 68 S.E. 2d 221—1951). Because of the reaction an animal may have when physically examined (or when being groomed or handled), the veterinarian (or other pet-care professional) should realize what actions may startle the animal. This requirement was set forth in Beck v. Henkle-Grain Livestock Co., where a veterinarian improperly secured a mule prior to an operation. The mule bolted, thereby receiving serious injuries, and the court held the veterinarian liable for failing to insure that the animal was properly restrained. Note the wording is "properly restrained." Although there are no cases involving the improper handling of dogs, the reasoning of the Beck case will apply to most such cases.

Since each dog can be expected to react differently to the grooming or boarding situation, kennel atmosphere, etc., the same yardstick can be applied in the event that a dog is injured during handling. In the Beck case the court ruled, in essence, that an experienced veterinarian should have known that the mule might try to bolt, and he was negligent in not anticipating that act. Even though the animal died as a result of its own actions, the veterinarian was still held responsible for *allowing* it to injure itself.

Likewise, kennel operators who fail to adequately restrain dogs in their custody could find themselves in the same boat if anything went wrong. As restraining equipment is available, and as such equipment is being used by a majority, anyone who chooses not to use safety restrainers could well be deemed negligent in the event of mishap.

To the best of my knowledge, most major legal suits have been settled out of court for an average settlement of $1,500 to $2,000 per dog. In several instances the dogs had died.

160

Legal Ramifications of Pet Owners Assisting Groomers

According to Murray Loring, DVM, JD, author of *Your Dog and the Law*:

> If a dog owner insists on holding his or her animal during a grooming session, nail trimmings, etc., and then is injured by the animal, legally you may be liable for the injury unless certain precautions were taken before you began the procedure.
>
> Whereas there are no laws or legal provisions that prevent owners from holding their dogs during such proceedings, there are important considerations to be aware of.
>
> Primarily, you should adequately warn the owner about the possibility of being scratched or bitten during the procedure. To this end, it would be advisable to require owners to sign a release form before being permitted to hold the animal. In situations where there are observers present, they also should sign a release form. The best safeguard, however, is to have neither holders nor observers present.
>
> If the owner cajoles you into being present, be it as holder or observer, a general release form (or one specifically designed by an attorney), signed by the dog's owner, should be standard operating procedure for those owners desirous of holding or observing their animals during the grooming or other service. Likewise, all other observers should be required to sign.
>
> If no warning is given and/or no release form signed, you may have to prove in court the following: the owner was experienced with dogs in general; the owner had held his or her canine on previous occasions while the animal was being groomed; and the owner held the animal contrary to clear and distinct orders.
>
> Further, the groomer or kennel operator may have to testify to the court that he or she had no knowledge the canine had a vicious propensity [dangerous trait] or history of biting or scratching. You may also have to convince the court that the owner had prior knowledge of the animal's dangerous trait, that you were not made aware of this fact. All the facts may have to be proved in court. If you are unable to do that, your chances of favorably persuading the court become more difficult.

The practice of permitting owners, or other individuals, to hold or witness the grooming of dogs contains the aforementioned pitfalls, in addition to the possibility of complaints that may arise from animal humane organizations. Owners assisting in grooming sessions, or mere observers, may report their conception of cruelty to these organizations. "Shocking one's sensibilities" could lead to a threat of legal action. If a groomer pays little or no heed to those who assist or observe during grooming, is unmindful of the effect it might have on "outsiders" in the room or, in fact, invites such participation or observation, then the groomer and kennel proprietor may be open to legal difficulties. The groomer is put on the defensive and has to expend valuable time denying such allegations—unfounded or otherwise.

Although groomers should not run scared about using owners to assist in holding their dogs or cats during grooming, since there are situations where this is helpful and reasonable, they should keep in mind that negligence or lack of foresight that might lead to an owner's injury may also lead them to the courtroom.

To minimize the risk of a legal confrontation, when owner-holders or observers are present during the grooming, the groomer should remember these key points: give ample, direct and clearly understood warnings; have release forms duly signed; refrain from negligence. Best of all, have a policy of not allowing owners to assist or observers to be present.

29

How to Live with the Law

It will be of little avail to the people that the laws are made by men of their choice if the laws be so voluminous that they cannot be read, or so incoherent that they cannot be understood: if they be repealed or revised before they are promulgated, or undergo such incessant changes that no man, who knows what the law is today, can guess what it will be tomorrow.

James Madison

UNFORTUNATELY, MOST KENNEL OWNERS consider legal services only when they or their business are in trouble. Legal troubles can be reduced or avoided by regular consultation, carried out on a continuing basis. The advice and suggestions of a lawyer concerning day-to-day operations can help prevent costly and time-consuming problems.

Your Lawyer's Value to You

A lawyer's job, properly performed, is to see that clients adhere to the law and thus prevent inadvertent violations that may prove costly. The legal services that a lawyer provides to the owner of a kennel or grooming business can be summarized in four words: checking, advising, guiding and representing.

Your lawyer can check past actions to determine if you have unintentionally violated the law.

In advising, the lawyer can explain the legal principles involved in the various courses of action that are open to you under the law.

163

A decision is easy to make when only one action is allowed, but judgment may be difficult when the law allows several courses of action. At this point a lawyer's guidance becomes valuable. While the ultimate decision is yours, the lawyer, because of his or her experience, can help evaluate the courses of action and assist in making decisions.

In representing the kennel or shop owner, the lawyer speaks as one specialist to other specialists. A lawyer knows and can talk the language of licensing boards, regulatory bodies, the courts and other governmental agencies. Equally important is the representation your lawyer provides in negotiating and drafting contracts. You can be sure your interest is protected, for example, when your lawyer sits down with his or her counterpart to negotiate a lease. A knowledgeable lawyer can protect you from unknowingly placing restrictions on future expansion plans or obligating yourself to pay the renovation costs if your rented facility is damaged by whatever cause.

Legal Guidance in Organizing a Business

The financial future of a service business is affected by the initial decision of the owner as to the form to be used in its organization. There are certain incidents attached to any form selected that make it imperative that an attorney discuss fully the consequences with the owner.

Three forms generally are available to the owner—sole ownership, partnership or a corporation. Each form has distinct rules applicable to it regarding taxation, management, liabilities of the owner and the division of profits, if any. Only after being advised as to all these options can an intelligent decision be made as to which is most suitable.

Legal services are a necessity when the choice of organization requires contracts, partnership agreements or the filing of other legal documents. There are local municipal and state law requirements attached to the beginning of any new business. Full compliance can be best assured with legal advice.

Even after the business is established, periodic checks should be made as the business progresses—particularly from a tax standpoint. For example, a sole proprietorship may have been desirable in the early years. However, when a firm grows and profits are increasing, the owner may desire to incorporate in order to obtain a tax advantage and at the same time reduce personal liability for any losses of the business. As management responsibilities increase, he or she may wish to form a partnership to help carry the load, or may wish to capitalize on the increasing value of the business by incorporating and selling shares in the business.

Legal Guidance in Acquiring Property

Acquiring property is another area in which legal services can be

164

helpful and profitable. This is true whether the property is real estate or merchandise.

In many cases a renter's concern with real estate is through a landlord. He or she rents space in which to operate a business. In such cases, a lawyer always should check the provisions of the lease. The lawyer can explain in lay language the consequences you may suffer because of provisions in a lease. Some of the more important considerations when signing a lease are: (1) title to and cost of any improvements to be made to the property, (2) ownership of these improvements when the lease ends, (3) renewal provisions, (4) any restriction on competitive operation by the lessee or others, (5) provisions as to compensation in case of fire or condemnation of the property, (6) provisions for assignment or subletting of the premises, and (7) the means of determining and measuring your sales—an important item when the amount of rent is to depend on a percentage of sales, such as in a shopping mall.

Your lawyer will also call to your attention any reciprocal restrictions as to the use of the premises that may be found in some leases.

If you buy a kennel building the services of a lawyer are essential. In those states where title abstract companies do not operate, a lawyer will examine and certify title to the real estate to insure that you will own what you are buying. Also, he or she can explain the meaning and impact of any mortgage or other type of instrument necessary to finance the purchase.

Buying Goods for Resale

If you buy a stock of merchandise from another retailer or another business, your lawyer can tell you whether you are complying with the applicable provisions of the Uniform Commercial Code or the Bulk Sales Law of the state in which you and the seller are located. Basically, these laws require that the creditors of the seller be protected in any outright sale of stock of merchandise to another. Your title to the goods may be jeopardized if you fail to examine and comply with these laws. Your lawyer can also check for any security interests that may be outstanding against the goods and insure that you have proper title before you close the transaction.

There are innumerable instances in which the advice of an attorney with tax experience is essential in complying with tax laws. Advice and assistance on such matters can be helpful not only when the business is showing profits but also when it has losses. For example, the effects of a loss when a newly established firm is trying to reach its break-even point sometimes may be softened measurably by using the loss in relation to other income (if any).

Employees

Obtaining advice and assistance on laws covering employees is

165

another helpful legal service. For example, a lawyer can point out and help you to observe the requirements that federal and state laws have on wages, employees' hours, workmen's compensation and unemployment compensation.

Litigation

Of course, you'll use a lawyer to defend you if someone should sue you or if you are otherwise involved in litigation. Such cases are often easier when you call on a lawyer who is familiar with your business. This familiarity, which your lawyer gets from working with you on a regular basis, can also enable him to help you prevent situations that might lead to legal hassles. Such preventive law can keep you and your business out of the court room so you can avoid time-consuming and expensive attempts to rescue a situation after things have gotten out of hand.

Handling Debt

Sometimes businesses get in trouble because they are unable to pay their debts. If things have not progressed too far, a lawyer may be able to work out an arrangement that will allow an owner to pay debts on an installment plan over an extended period of time and out of current income. In other cases, the lawyer may help to reorganize your financial structure so that creditors can receive a reasonable amount of repayment while the business continues to operate. On the other hand, if the creditors insist on closing, the lawyer can prevent creditors from taking unfair advantage of the situation and insulate the client from any undue personal liability for the debts of the business.

Selling the Business

Legal services can be helpful if for any reason you want to sell your business as a going operation or dispose of all or substantially all the assets of your business.

Many tax and credit implications are involved in the disposition of assets. The advice and assistance of a lawyer can help you to avoid premature taxation. It can also insure that no personal liability is imposed on you in the transfer of the assets.

As a rule, the purchase or sale of a business or of a substantial part of a business requires the seller to provide certain covenants, warranties and representations as to the title and quality of the merchandise and property being transferred. When made in a legally correct way these representations protect both seller and buyer. Without legal counsel, intentionally or otherwise, such contracts and warranties may eventually prove to be unreasonable and unjust to one or other of the parties involved.

166

30

Self-Employment Standards for Groomers and Kennel Owners

K ENNEL OWNERS MAY PREFER to rent space to independent groomers instead of maintaining their own grooming operation and employing someone to groom for them. After making inquiries with several Internal Revenue Service (IRS) departments, the following information was provided by a district director with the IRS: Because there are no set precedents for dog groomers they will be governed by the same standards as are already established for barbers, beauticians and manicurists.

The determination as to whether or not an employer-employee relationship exists is often very difficult and usually must be done on a case-by-case basis. Some of the factors that should be considered are (1) does the groomer provide his own equipment, (2) is the groomer free to refuse service to a customer, (3) does he regulate his own working hours, (4) does he perform services other than grooming and (5) is the groomer required to groom the dog in accordance with the kennel owner's instructions. In addition to this list, there is a list of 20 common law factors that can be used to determine the existence of an employer-employee relationship.

The Internal Revenue Service has issued no revenue rulings concerning the employer-employee relationship between professional dog groomers and kennel owners. However, it has issued rulings for beauticians, manicurists and barbers where, although the type of work is different, the facts are similar. After reading these rulings, you will see that in some instances there will be an employer-employee relationship between the groomer and the kennel owner and in some cases there will not.

If an employer-employee relationship exists, the kennel owner would be responsible for withholding and paying the Federal Withholding Tax and the payroll taxes. If there is no employer-employee relationship, the groomer would be responsible for making estimated tax payments if necessary and for paying self-employment taxes.

The national office of the Internal Revenue Service has the authority to issue revenue rulings. If you want a revenue ruling concerning the employer-employee relationship between professional dog groomers and kennel owners, please address your request to:

> Commissioner of the Internal Revenue Service
> Attention: R:PS:T
> 1111 Constitution Ave. N.W.
> Washington, D.C. 20224

The Factors or Elements That Show Control Under the Common Law Test, or Employee-Employer Relationship

1. A person who is required to comply with instructions is ordinarily an employee.
2. Training of a person by an experienced employee working with him, by correspondence or by required attendance at meetings, indicates control.
3. Integration of the person's services in the business operations generally shows that he is subject to direction and control.
4. If the services must be rendered personally it indicates that the employer is interested in the methods as well as the results.
5. Hiring, supervising and payment of assistants by the employer generally shows control over all the men and women on the job.
6. The existence of a continuing relationship between an individual and the person for whom he performs services is a factor tending to indicate the existence of an employer-employee relationship.
7. The establishment of set hours of work by the employer is a factor indicative of control.
8. If the worker must devote his full time to the business of the employer, it implies control.
9. Doing the work on the employer's premises is not control in itself; however, it does imply that the employer has control.
10. If a person must perform services in the order or sequence set for him by the employer, it shows that the worker is not free to follow his own pattern of work.

11. If regular oral or written reports must be submitted to the employer, it indicates control.
12. Payment for work by the hour, week or month is usually the manner for paying employees, whereas payment on a commission or job basis is customary where the worker is an independent contractor.
13. Payment by the employer of the worker's business and/or traveling expense is a factor indicating control over the worker.
14. The furnishing of tools, materials, etc., by the employer is indicative of control over the worker. *Materials is the most important factor.*
15. A significant investment by a person in facilities used by him in performing services for another tends to show an independent status.
16. A person who is in a position to realize a profit or suffer a loss as a result of his services is generally an independent contractor.
17. If a person works for a number of persons or firms at the same time, it usually indicates an independent status because in such cases the worker is usually free from control by any of the firms.
18. The fact that a person makes his services available to the general public is usually indicative of an independent contractual relationship.
19. The right to discharge is an important factor in indicating that the person possessing the right is an employer.
20. An employee has the right to end his relationship with his employer at any time he wishes without incurring liability.

Who Are Employees?

An individual is an employee for federal employment tax purposes if he has the status of an employee under the usual common law rules applicable in determining the employer-employee relationship. Guides for determining whether that relationship exists are found in three substantially similar sections of the Employment Tax Regulations, namely, sections 31.3121(d)-1, 31.3306(i)-1, and 31.3401(c)-1. Generally, the relationship of employer and employee exists when the person for whom the services are performed has the right to control and direct the individual who performs the services not only as to the result to be accomplished by the work but also as to the details and means by which that result is accomplished.

Example 1. A manicurist performing services in a barbershop who, under an agreement with the barbershop operator, is free to refuse service to any patron, regulates her working hours, furnishes her own equipment and supplies, collects and retains the proceeds from her work and may terminate the arrangement whenever it is no longer satisfactory, is not an employee of the operator for purposes of FICA, FUTA, and income tax withholding but is engaged in a "trade of business" for self-employment tax purposes.

Example 2. Under an agreement with the operator of a barbershop a manicurist obligated herself to furnish a manicuring service to the patrons of the shop during the hours that the shop is open for business. However, it was stipulated that no such service would be furnished on Wednesdays. The service agreed upon consisted of the availability of a skilled and competent manicurist, either the party to the agreement or some other qualified individual selected by her and acceptable to the shop operator. The manicurist is free to refuse to perform the manicuring services to any patron of the shop if she so chooses. She regulates her own hours, furnishes her own equipment, tools, instruments and supplies required in the conduct of her business and collects and retains the proceeds from her work without using the operator's cash register or otherwise furnishing the operator of the shop information concerning her income. While she is not required to and does not secure the operator's approval when she takes a vacation, as a matter of courtesy she does advise the operator prior to leaving for an extended absence. The arrangement may be terminated by either party when it is no longer satisfactory.

The facts in this case show that the manicurist has only obligated herself to furnish a service to patrons of the shop operator. She did not agree that she would personally perform the services and, in fact, retains the right to employ someone else for this purpose. The agreement between the manicurist and the operator does not give the operator the right to direct the manner in which these services are to be performed. The only right that the operator has in the event of unsatisfactory performance is to terminate the arrangement. Although the operator does have that right and does furnish the place to work, these factors are not sufficient to establish the relationship of employer and employee between the operator and the manicurist.

In this case, the operator does not exercise, or have the right to exercise, over the manicurist the degree of direction and control necessary to establish the employer-employee relationship. Accordingly, the manicurist is not an employee of the operator for purposes of the Federal Insurance Contributions Act, the Federal Unemployment Tax Act, or the Collection of Income Tax at Source on Wages. She is self-employed.

Example 3. Under an agreement with a beauty salon a beautician agrees to "lease" a space in the salon to be used for the sole purpose of performing services as a beautician and hairdresser. The salon agrees to furnish, repair, and maintain all of the equipment, materials, supplies, accessories and personal tools usually used in the operation of a beauty salon. For her services the beautician receives a specified percentage of all money taken in by her. No credit or free work may be done by the

170

beautician without the prior express approval of the salon. The agreement may be terminated by either party upon one week's notice.

The salon rules require the beautician to be at her chair at 8 A.M. on those days that she is scheduled to work, to furnish her own uniforms, to charge fees as determined by the salon, and to perform services as requested by the customers. The beautician furnishes a report each day to the owner reflecting the day's receipts. The salon uses these records as the basis for computing the amount due to her. The beautician is required to work until 6 P.M. on weekdays and until noon on Saturday. The beautician obtains the necessary licenses for cosmetology from the state and pays the appropriate fees.

The facts in this case show that the beauty salon has the right to direct and control the beautician in the performance of her services, not only as to the result to be accomplished by the work but also as to the details and means by which that result is accomplished. Accordingly, the beautician is considered an employee of the beauty salon for purposes of the Federal Insurance Contributions Act, the Federal Unemployment Tax Act, and the Collection of Income Tax at Source on Wages.

Example 4. Under an agreement with a beauty salon, a beautician agrees to rent, for a fixed monthly fee, a booth containing a hydraulic chair, dressing table, storage space and mirror. In addition, the salon furnishes heat, light, water and the usual beautician supplies. The beautician's primary activities consist of selling and styling wigs that she purchases herself and she receives from such activities. In addition, she works on the salon's customers from time to time, although she is not required to do so. She does not receive any guaranteed amount from the salon. The beautician is free to select her own customers, set her own work schedule and to come and go as she pleases. The beautician does not have to report for work at a specific hour or work a stated number of hours per day or week.

The shop rules require her to be responsible for cleaning her own work area, to maintain her own tools and to furnish and maintain her own uniforms. The beautician obtains the necessary licenses for cosmetology from the state and pays the appropriate fees.

The facts in this case show that the beauty salon, in entering into the fixed-fee lease agreement with the individual in question, makes the services of an additional beautician available, both for its convenience and for the convenience of its customers. While furnishing a place to work and supplies are factors to be considered in determining an employer-employee relationship, the existence of those factors alone is not sufficient to establish such a relationship for federal employment tax purposes.

In this case, the beauty salon does not exercise, or have the right to exercise, over the beautician the degree of direction and control necessary to establish the employer-employee relationship. Accordingly, the beautician is not an employee of the beauty salon for purposes of the Federal Insurance Contributions Act, the Federal Unemployment Tax Act, or the Collection of Income Tax at Source on Wages. She is self-employed.

Example 5. A barber pays a shop owner (also a barber) a regular weekly rental for the use of a chair in his shop. In addition to the chair, the owner furnishes heat, light, water and all of the usual barber supplies, such as towels, lotions and soap. The individual furnishes his own tools of the trade and has obtained a license in his own name from the state board of barber examiners. He determines his own work routine and is not required to perform a minimum amount of work nor to be on duty a specific number of hours per day or week. Because of the nature of his services, he naturally has an established route in order to be available for customers desiring his services. All fees collected by him for his services are retained by him and no accounting of such collections is made to the shop owner. While the individual has no set hours for his work, he usually tries to arrange his absences from the shop to occur at times when the shop owner is present, in consideration and for the convenience of the customers. The agreement may be terminated by either party at any time upon proper notice.

In this case the individual is not subject to such direction and control by the barber shop owner as is necessary, under the usual common law rules, to establish an employer-employee relationship for federal employment tax purposes. Accordingly, the individual is not an employee of the shop owner for purposes of the Federal Insurance Contributions Act. He is self-employed.

Any arrangement between a kennel owner and a dog groomer acting as a private contractor must meet the same criteria as exists for barbers, beauticians and manicurists. The above examples may be useful as guides for determining whether the employer-employee relationship exists. For specific clarification, consult your local IRS office.

172

APPENDIX

Innovative Kennels

The Monolithic Dome

The so-called monolithic dome looks more like a concrete igloo than a kennel building. Its construction cost and overall efficiency suggest that this type of structure has the potential to become the kennel design of the future; however, the dome design originated in Idaho, where it is used primarily for potato storage. Elsewhere it is becoming widely used for grain and other crop storage.

The first dome kennel was built in Greely, Colorado, in 1980 to house the Humane Society of Weld County. The cost was approximately $35 per square foot, compared to $50-plus for a conventional building of similar capacity. The total cost of the 8,659 square-foot facility was $253,000. Although the unit cost has increased in keeping with inflation, the dome remains an economically sound idea and several similar units are being constructed in Florida and other areas of the country.

The term "monolithic" suggests that the dome resembles a solid hunk of rock and seems quite appropriate under the circumstances. The building, although obviously not solid, is in actuality a one-piece concrete structure and has no beams, pillars or other supports.

The dome is insulated with a three-inch urethane exterior coating, plus elastomatic polyethelene for extra protection. It has an R-factor of R25; its K-factor is a stingy .14 BTUs or less of heat transfer. The heating plant is equipped with a recoil heat system that prewarms frigid incoming air. The average monthly utility costs for 1984 were $425 for 7,523 kwh of power and $260 for 596 cubic ft. of gas.

While the virtually airtight design is essential to the dome's economical operation, especially during the harsh Colorado winters, this could conceivably present a problem with disease control. However, that is effectively resolved with an air filtration system that turns the air over approximately 12 times every hour.

The Weld County Humane Society Shelter is 105 feet in diameter (the largest available dome is 200 feet), with a total capacity of 220 animals. This includes 42 inside runs, office space, storage and all essential support facilities. For additional space, if needed, a second floor can be incorporated into the design or satellite buildings can be added around the main structure.

Kennelwood Village

Kennelwood Village is a completely new pet-care complex located in St. Louis, Missouri. Its location, facilities and equipment were designed to make it a model of contemporary pet care, offering the highest standards in comfort, nutrition, security, sanitation and individualized services. These services include private and group training from puppy to advanced classes, in-home training, problem counseling, dog and cat grooming, ID tattooing, a flea and tick control program, hot oil treatment, day-care service, a complete line of pet supplies, pick-up and delivery, pet shipping and travel service, "playschool" and a puppy selection process that allows prospective buyers to meet and talk with reputable breeders.

The inside pens are brightly painted and floors are covered with cushioned antifatigue flooring. The building is air conditioned for year-round comfort and piped-in music helps keep boarders calm and quiet. For added safety the complex is protected by a security fence, with a resident attendant on hand keeping a watchful eye on the proceedings at all times.

Cats have the option of 1-, 2-, or 3-level condos and the use of "Little Cat Country"—a large exercise area where they can climb trees, work out on scratching posts, play with catnip toys or simply lounge on cat furniture.

The playschool program affords dogs the added benefits of using the playschool fun course, which provides them with the daily exercise, grooming, petting and personalized attention they'd receive at home. A report card is provided to appraise each dog's owner of its reaction to the playschool concept.

Preston Country Club for Pets

This kennel, built on 16 acres in 1966 and expanded in 1976 to house 140 dogs and 35 cats, serves the Washington, D.C. area.

The main kennel is a square, cinderblock building that is cheerfully illuminated by skylights and fluorescent lighting. Of symmetrical design, the kennel consists of double-decked pens on all four outside walls, each of

176

The monolithic dome—a seamless, freestanding, concrete structure primarily intended for storage purposes—converts into an ideal kennel facility. It is especially useful in areas of the country like Colorado and Florida where the elements are extreme enough to create the need for maximum year-round protection. The interior of the dome can be subdivided to suit specific requirements using concrete block, wood frame construction or a combination of both. Extra space is obtained by adding a second floor or using smaller satellite buildings.

Kennelwood Village

PLAYSCHOOL REPORT CARD for

_____

_____

FUN COURSE SUBJECTS	GRADES
Walking and running on leash	
Playing Ball	
Petting	
Brushing	
Behavior	
Cooperated with Teacher	
Friendly with Other Students	

Teacher's comments: _____

_____

_____

_____

TEACHER_____

Except for home
your pet never had it so good!

Kennelwood Village supplies a "report card" that appraises the dog's behavior.

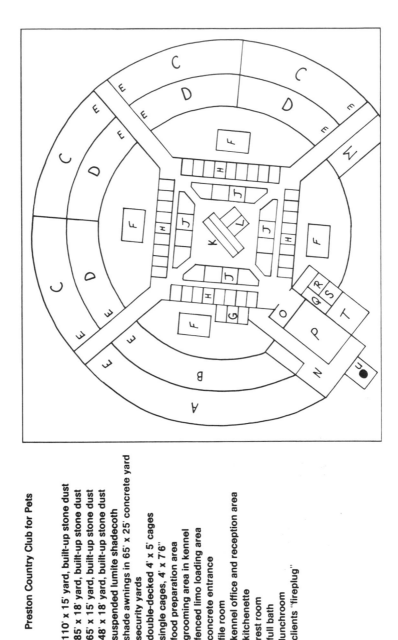

Preston Country Club for Pets

A. 110' x 15' yard, built-up stone dust
B. 85' x 18' yard, built-up stone dust
C. 65' x 15' yard, built-up stone dust
D. 48' x 18' yard, built-up stone dust
E. suspended lumite shadecoth
F. shade awnings in 65' x 25' concrete yard
G. security yards
H. double-decked 4' x 5' cages
J. single cages, 4' x 7'6"
K. food preparation area
L. grooming area in kennel
M. fenced limo loading area
N. concrete entrance
O. file room
P. kennel office and reception area
Q. kitchenette
R. rest room
S. full bath
T. lunchroom
U. clients "fireplug"

A schematic of the Preston Country Club for Pets.

178

which has its own 16 ft. × 16 ft. plate-glass window. There are also four rows of single cages on the inside, facing inward. The center of the kennel, which contains the kitchen and the boarders' grooming and bathing facilities, is utilized as a work area so that the animals are never isolated from the staff.

Each boarder is groomed at least twice during its stay. The average stay is seven to ten days. Those staying for longer periods also receive a weekly nine-point health check.

The bi-level pens, constructed of concrete blocks, are 4 ft. × 5 ft; the upper tier is four feet high and the bottom one six inches lower. The dimensions of the inner pens are 4 ft. × 7½ ft.

Spacious exercise yards literally surround the kennel. The largest are a substantial 115 ft. × 15 ft. in size; the smallest are 48 ft. × 18 ft. All the dogs are systematically rotated from their pens to the exercise runs twice daily.

Only four runs are made of concrete; the remainder are gravel. The gravel, which is eight inches deep and topped with stone-dust, is replaced periodically, as it is worn down from all the scooping that occurs. Gravel runs are sanitized using a combination of lime and rock-salt and sprayed with bleach.

A recent addition houses the cattery, office, reception room and merchandizing area. Cats are confined in Shorline cages and exercised in the cat jungle room. Twice weekly their nails are trimmed, eyes and ears checked and they are petromalted to prevent hairballs.

The size of the kennel staff needed to provide the necessary attention to the boarders varies in number from 14 to 24 full- and part-time employees.

Customers freely avail themselves of the limousine pick-up service. The limo is operated as a separate business and is made available to other area kennels.

To avoid paying a two-day penalty, anyone cancelling a reservation during the busy season must give 48 hours notice.

The grooming shop, which employs three full-time groomers and a part-time bather, is located in a separate building.

Kennel Plans

THE KENNEL PLANS and materials specifications outlined in this section are self-explanatory. If you are planning a large commercial venture you can reduce costs by shopping around for the best bids on materials, labor and financing.

As interim financing interest may be computed on a day-to-day basis, it is important that contractors and subcontractors failing to meet agreed deadlines be required to pay substantial penalties. Hire a lawyer to protect your interests and never sign so-called "standard" contracts without the benefit of legal advice.

Good construction is square and plumb throughout. Spend as much time at the site as possible, keep your eyes and ears open and question everything that does not conform to specifications.

When planning a kennel it is important to choose your materials carefully. While the majority of prospective kennel builders are most concerned with the initial cost of the project, it is prudent to remember that low operating expenses and easy maintenance are equally important in the long run.

A structure, whether for hobby or commercial use, must be durable, provide maximum comfort for its occupants, and be fireproof, easily sanitized and readily expandable.

For maximum durability, concrete block construction and steel fence posts should be used in preference to wood. Generally speaking, wooden gates and fence posts are not a good investment. Being porous they absorb moisture and odor, are prone to dry rot and termites and susceptible to chewing and clawing damage. In soil with high acid content even the best wood rarely lasts more than five years. Although wood can be treated with a variety of sealers or protective coatings, when you stop to compare the overall costs there is little or nothing to choose between wood and steel. So why bother?

The interior of wood-frame buildings can be kept relatively fireproof by minimizing the use of combustible materials and encasing all electrical cable in metal conduit. The condition of the electrical wiring is especially important if you are converting an older structure. Beware of aluminum electrical installations erected during the 1960s. Aluminum cable has been linked to numerous electrical fires and its use has been discontinued, but many of the old, potentially hazardous installations still exist.

Large block buildings should have firewalls at appropriate intervals and self-closing steel doors so that a fire outbreak cannot spread rapidly throughout the entire facility. Smoke alarms are a good investment for any building.

Sound-proofing is another frequently overlooked feature. The use of adequate insulation and acoustical ceiling tile helps achieve noise reduction. Some kennels tend to amplify barking and noise in general, which can lead to noise-related stress for both dogs and humans.

Building materials and methods are constantly being improved and upgraded, so it pays to review one's options carefully during the intial planning stages. Buying prefabricated modular runs, for example, may be cheaper than the labor cost of having them constructed at the site. Modular construction, based on using standard 8 ft. × 4 ft. sheets of building material, also helps reduce labor costs.

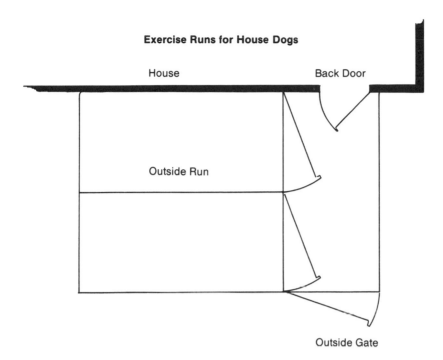

Exercise Runs for House Dogs

House

Back Door

Outside Run

Outside Gate

The convenience of safe outdoor enclosures are as beneficial for dogs living in the home as for those housed in kennels. This plan permits safe access to the outdoors and then to the individual runs. Here, care should be taken that the outside gate is securely closed before the back door from the house is opened.

Most Popular Small Kennel Layout for Basements, Garages or Existing Buildings

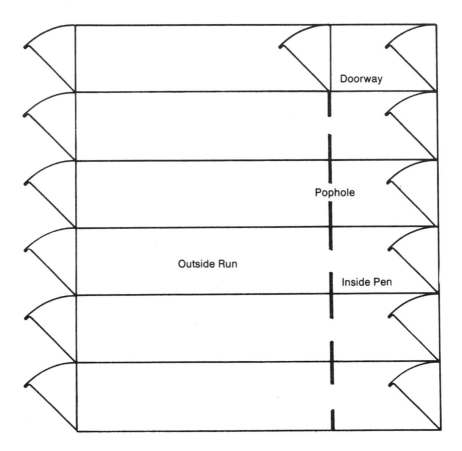

Doorway

Pophole

Outside Run

Inside Pen

When kennel facilities are built into a portion of the home or designed to fit an existing building, getting the maximum use out of a small space is often the rule. Such a design demands compactness with efficiency within the confines of the physical plant.

Exercise Area for House Dogs

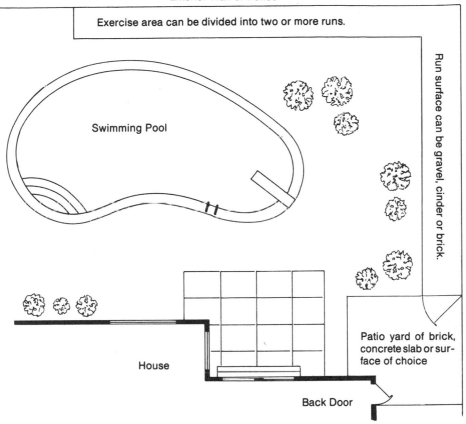

Exterior Wall or Fence

Exercise area can be divided into two or more runs.

Swimming Pool

Run surface can be gravel, cinder or brick.

House

Patio yard of brick, concrete slab or surface of choice

Back Door

When there is sufficient running room on a property, many home owners like to construct a long, narrow run inside one or more sides of the outside fence or wall. This plan also includes a small paddock furnishing the dogs a totally useful and comfortable outdoor environment.

Dirt or gravel runs under shade trees

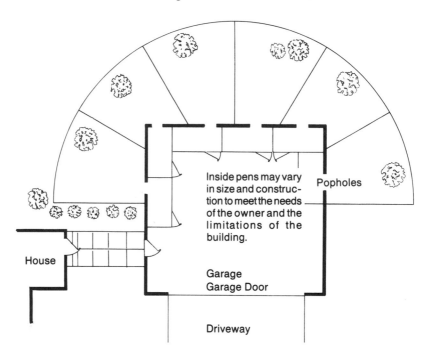

Inside pens may vary in size and construction to meet the needs of the owner and the limitations of the building.

Popholes

House

Garage
Garage Door

Driveway

When a kennel is to be made from a converted garage, the building itself and surrounding land will dictate much of the physical form. A design that takes advantage of both building and land will make for the most useful facility.

Boarding Kennel or Hospital
Inside Runs—Alternative Design.
May Also be Used as Holding Pens

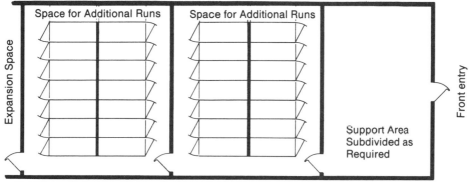

Dividing walls may be constructed of block, wood, wire or party solid topped with wire.

Boarding Kennel or Veterinary Hospital
Combination Using Pens or Cages and Indoor Runs
Also Suitable combined with Stacked Cages

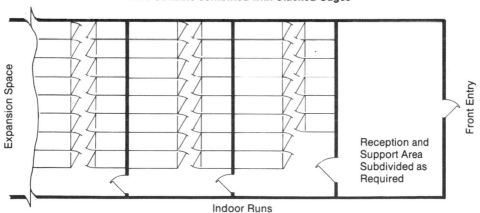

Indoor Runs

Indoor Pens or Cages

Boarding Kennel

Main Entry

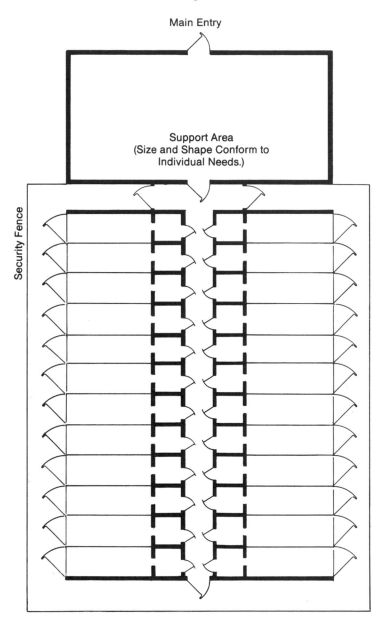

Support Area
(Size and Shape Conform to
Individual Needs.)

Security Fence

This is the floor plan most popular for boarding kennels which feature outdoor runs attached to indoor sleeping areas for each dog.

188

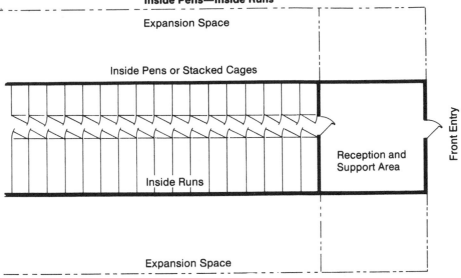

Boarding Kennel or Veterinary Hospital
Inside Pens—Inside Runs

Expansion Space

Inside Pens or Stacked Cages

Inside Runs

Reception and
Support Area

Front Entry

Expansion Space

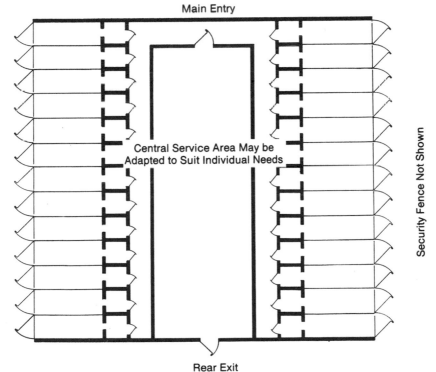

Alternative Design
Main Entry

Central Service Area May be
Adapted to Suit Individual Needs

Security Fence Not Shown

Rear Exit

This design can serve the needs of a boarding kennel, veterinary hospital, handler's show
kennel or private hobby facility.

189

Sample Contracts

ANY SERVICE BUSINESS involving the handling of animals by other than their owners calls for the careful use of written contracts. Earlier in this book numerous examples were given of legal actions arising out of the unexpected in business dealings between owners of animals and those professionals who furnish services most owners cannot or will not give.

Contracts which spell out specifics with regard to reasonable care, why the animal is being turned over to another party, costs and all other questions bearing on the transaction should be spelled out. Trouble is easily avoided when all parties understand their mutual obligations prior to accepting a pet for veterinary treatment, boarding, grooming, training or showing. Any potential risks to the health and even the life of the animal should also be carefully delineated before any agreement is signed.

Several examples of contracts are reproduced in this section for your reference. If you deal with the animal-owning public, written contracts are a necessity. Of course, the form of the contracts you use and what they contain will depend on your business and the range of services you intend to provide.

Don't assume dealings with clientele will always go smoothly; remember "Murphy's Law" and make allowance for the unexpected. Before opening your doors, speak to a competent business lawyer and be guided accordingly. Once someone's pet is accidentally injured, killed or escapes while in your care it will be too late to wish you had. . . . Determine your needs and operate with legally binding, written instruments at all times. To do less is to invite disaster.

191

BOARDING CONTRACT

DATE: _____ (READ BEFORE SIGNING)

Name of Dog or Cat: _____

Received this date from: _____ Owner/or _____

Address: _____ Phone _____

_____Dog(s) _____ Cat(s) Breed _____

Sex _____ Age _____ Color _____ License No. _____

Owner attaches herewith proof of current rabies immunization, distemper, hepatitis-lepto and canine cough shots as required by Orange County Ordinances.

Does Animal: Bite _____   Jump _____   Climb _____   Has Animal Been boarded before? _____

Approx. date of last inoculation for: Rabies _____   Distemper _____   Hepatitis _____   Leptospirosis _____

Has animal ever had: Skin Trouble? _____   Feline Distemper? _____   In case of illness call _____

This Animal is here for _____(days) (weeks) (months)   at the rate of $_____ per (day) (week) (month) payable in advance on the first day of each (week) (month) until called for.

1. The _____ hereinafter referred to as the "Kennel", agrees to exercise due and reasonable care to keep its premises sanitary and property enclosed.

2. The Kennel does not assume and shall not be held responsible for any liability with respect to the animal listed in this agreement, of any kind, character, or nature whatsoever, arising out of or from the boarding of this animal, or any damages which may accrue from any other cause whatsoever, including loss by fire, theft, running away, death, injury to persons, animals, or property, or death or injury to any other animal caused by the within named animal during the term of this contract, whether this animal be on the premises of the Kennel or not, and the owner of said animal agrees hereby to be and is solely responsible for any and all acts of behavior of said animal at any time within the term and time of the contract. In no case shall the Kennel be in any way liable or responsible. The responsibility and/or liability of the Kennel, in no event shall exceed the sum of One Hundred Dollars ($100.00) and the undersigned agrees to limit the responsibility against One Hundred Dollars ($100.00) for any and all damages sustained or suffered by reason of the boarding of this animal with said Kennel to the sum of One Hundred Dollars ($100.00) and no more, and agrees not to claim any damages against siad Kennel of any nature whatsoever, either by way of contract, equity, negligence or otherwise, in excess of said sum.

3. The owner of the within named animal specifically represents that he is the sole owner of said animal and that there is not now any lien or mortgage against said animal and that the within named animal has not been exposed to distemper or rabies within the last thirty days, and that the required annual license has been obtained.

4. The Kennel shall have, and is hereby granted, a lien on the aforesaid animal for any and all unpaid boarding and/or other charges resulting from the boarding of said animal with the Kennel. The owner hereby agrees that in the event that the monthly or weekly boarding charges are not paid within thirty days after they become due and payable in accordance with the terms of this contract, the Kennel may exercise its lien rights, and ten days after notice to owner may dispose of said animal for any and all unpaid charges, at private or public sale, and owner specifically waives sections 3051 and 3052 of the California Civil Code, and if such sale does not secure a price adequate to pay such costs of board and/or other charges delinquent plus costs of sale, then owner shall and must pay to Kennel the difference. Any monies realized by the Kennel at such a sale, over and above charges due and costs of sale shall be returned to Owner. Notice shall be conclusively deemed to have been given pursuant to this paragraph if notice in writing of such intended sale shall be mailed by registered mail to the owner of the within named animal at the address given herein, and no further notice shall be required.

5. If the animal becomes ill, the owner shall be notified at once, collect, if possible, or such attempt shall be made to so notify the owner, and if owner does not immediately inform the Kennel regarding measures to be taken or if the state of the animal's health requires quick action, the right to call a veterinarian or to administer medicine or to give advisable attention within the discretion shall be taken for granted by Kennel, and such expenses being reasonable in amount shall be promptly paid by owner.

6. Unless owner files with Kennel within thirty days from the date the animal is removed from the Kennel, a written demand for any claimed injury or damages resulting from the boarding of said animal under this contract, said owner shall and does hereby waive any and all rights which he may have against the Kennel for any liability arising under this contract for damages, or otherwise.

7. The singular, as herein used, means also the plural, the masculine gender means also feminine gender. If any word, sentence, or section of this agreement is declared invalid, such ruling shall nevertheless not affect any other word, sentence or section. The remedies hereunder are cumulative to Kennel and not alternative. No person is authorized by Kennel to change or waive any of the terms or conditions of this contract and Kennel will not be bound by any changes therein, whether oral or written. All terms and conditions of this agreement shall be binding on the heirs, administrators, and assigns of the owner of the within named animal. Time is of the essence hereof.

8. If anction is instituted by Kennel in order to enforce this contract, owner promises to pay such sum as the Court may fix as attorney's fees.

9. The animal is not to be taken off premises except by consent of the owner.

10. The owner guarantees payment of this bill. If for any reason this bill is not paid when presented, and is placed in the hands of an attorney for collection, the owner agrees that a reasonable fee may be added for attorney's fees, and other such costs as the court may allow. Interest charged on overdue bills are at the rate of 9%.

OWNER HEREBY ACKNOWLEDGES HAVING READ THIS CONTRACT

OWNER _____ BY _____

RECEIPT BY OWNER UPON RETURN OF ANIMAL: Owner acknowledges that he has taken possession of the within named animal in good condition from the Kennel this date.

DATED: _____ OWNER: _____

192

GROOMING CONTRACT

GROOMING DEPARTMENT
LAST NAME_____ **PHONE**_____
ADDRESS_____ **CITY**_____ **ZIP CODE**_____
CAT/DOG'S NAME_____ **BREED**_____ **COLOR**_____
BIRTH_____ **SPECIAL MARKINGS**_____

All pets boarded, or otherwise handled or cared for by _____ without liability for loss or damage from disease, death, running, or flying away, theft, injury to persons or other pets or property by said pet or other unavoidable causes, the above firm agrees to exercise due and reasonable care while pet is in its custody. If pet becomes ill, _____ Kennels, is hereby authorized in its discretion to call the veterinarian designated by owner. If the owner has not informed the firm of the name of the veterinarian and, in the opinion of the firm, the pet requires prompt medical attention, this firm is authorized to call a veterinarian or to give other advisable attention within the discretion of _____ Kennels and such expense, being reasonable in amount, shall be paid promptly by the owner of the pet. The owner represents that he is the legal owner of said pet, that said pet is not mortgaged in any way, and that said pet has not been exposed to distemper, enteritis, or other communicable diseases, within the last 30 days.
If pet is not called for within 10 days after time for return of pet, unless other suitable arrangements are made, the pet becomes property of firm boarding said pet.
The owner guarantees payment of this bill. If for any reason this bill is not paid when presented and is placed in the hand of any attorney for collection, the owner agrees that a reasonable fee may be added for attorney's fees, and such other costs as the court may allow. Interest charged on overdue bills at the rate of nine (9) percent.
This agreement may be terminated by either party at any time by giving written notice in person or by registered mail.

DATE_____ ACCEPTED_____
                                    Owner/Agent of Pet

DATE	PATTERN AND NOTES	DEB.	CR.	BAL.	GROOMER

DOG'S PROFILE

OWNER'S NAME_____

ADDRESS_____

PHONE (home)_____(business)_____

VETERINARIAN_____

VET'S PHONE_____

DOG'S NAME_____(AGE)_____

MEDICATION_____(WHAT KIND)_____

WHEN LAST GROOMED_____(REACTION)_____

WAS THE DOG GROOMED BY PROFESSIONAL_____OWNER_____

HOW OFTEN IS THE DOG GROOMED(BRUSHED, BATHED) AT HOME_____

HEALTH PROBLEMS

Seizures_____Specify_____
Heart Disease_____Specify_____
Blind_____Deaf_____Injuries_____
Allergies_____What Kind_____Ear Infection_____
Others_____

DOES DOG RESPOND TO NAME WHEN CALLED_____

IS DOG HOUSETRAINED_____

HOW DOES DOG REACT TO STRANGERS_____

DOES DOG URINATE WHEN APPROACHED_____

DOES DOG INDULGE IN SELF-MUTILATION_____

DOES DOG RESPOND TO OWNERS DIRECTION_____

IN STRESS SITUATION(new situation, strangers, left alone, confinement)
DOES DOG REACT:
Wildly Active_____Active_____Poised, Assured_____Reserved_____
Withdrawn (lethargic, stiff)_____

HAS DOG BITTEN ANYONE_____ WHAT WERE CIRCUMSTANCES_____
_____

WHO ADMINISTERS PUNISHMENT_____

WHAT TYPE OF PUNISHMENT_____

Helpful Kennel Items

THE FOLLOWING ITEMS are a sampling of noteworthy products on the market designed to aid owners and workers in the pet-care business.

The **D'flea® Liquid Dispensing Comb** (Texas Romec, Inc.) is an innovative and economical way of applying pesticides and hair-care products to the coat of long-haired breeds. The comb's teeth are fabricated of a porous nylon fiber, similar to that used for felt-tip pens, which allows even product distribution down to the skin.

The **Dog Care® First Aid Kit** (Pet Medical & Health Products, Inc.) for pet and kennel owners was developed by a veterinarian. It contains the basic essentials for emergency first-aid treatment and includes easy-to-follow, step-by-step instructions. It belongs in every kennel, grooming shop or other pet-care facility.

The **Shampro 2000® Automatic Pet Washing System** (Aweco) eliminates the need for time-consuming handling and mixing of shampoos, coat conditioners and pesticides. It allows easier, faster and more efficient bathing, parasite control and coat care in general. It is an ideal item for establishments that insist on mandatory dipping for their boarders.

Ultra-Board® and **Ultra-Board SP® Nonasbestos Panels** (Brit-Am) are weather resistant, almost industructible, fireproof building panels that seem ideally suited to many forms of kennel construction. They come in a reasonably attractive gray, which can be painted the color of your choice. This is viable alternative to block construction for the do-it-yourselfer. Available from all participating Weyerhaeuser customer service centers, it comes in 4 ft. × 8 ft. and 4 ft. × 10 ft. panels, ranging from $\frac{1}{8}$ to $\frac{1}{2}$ inch thick.

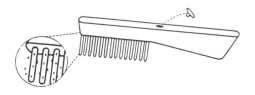

D'Flea® Liquid Dispensing Comb

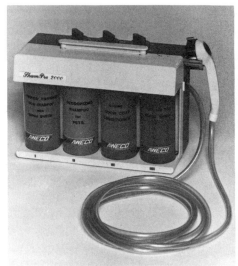

Shampro 2000© Automatic Pet Washing System

Ferrox Nonslip Floor Coating

Ultra-Board® Nonasbestos Panels

Super Cageliner (Clark-Cote Ltd. of Canada) is a sturdy, chew-resistant plastic cage liner or matting. It helps to reduce the incidence of decubious ulcers (pressure sores) on elbows and hocks of susceptible breeds like Great Danes and Dobes and protects Cocker and Poodle coats by keeping them dry and clean. It has a variety of other useful kennel applications.

Ferrox Nonslip Floor Coating (Martex Safety Prod.) comes in a variety of colors and is easily applied to provide better traction and reduce the danger of dogs and handlers slipping on slick surfaces. It provides both high- and low-profile protection, depending on the choice of application.

The **Quick Release Leash** (A.W. McNicoll, DVM) is a two-way nylon slip-lead that provides a safe way of handling obstreperous boarders. It works equally well with friendly animals. The double loop construction allows the handler to restrain and then release dogs with a minimum risk of personal injury.

The **Skitty Witty® Feline Domicile** is the ultimate in ultradeluxe cat housing. It comes with all the basic and not so basic necessities, including a litter box, feed dishes and even a waterbed, if desired. On the outside it looks like a TV or stereo console. It is the ultimate in pet pampering for those who care enough to want the very best!

The **Grooming Noose** and **Tub Tie** (Custom Cable) is an indestructible, chew-proof, plastic-coated steel restraining loop that provides added security. The Ear Cleaner Dispenser dispenses the ear cleaning liquid of your choice on cotton swabs without waste.

The **Fogmaster®** (Fogmaster Corp.) is from a line of hand-held and drum-service foggers designed to fit every kennel need. This provides a useful method of controlling insects and external parasites where such control is indicated.

The **Chemilizer® Q-2 Quaterinary Ammonia** and/or **Chlorine Dispenser** (Chemilizer Products, Inc.) proportionately dispenses selected disinfectants for optimum kennel sanitization. The **Pet Washer** attaches to the regular water supply and holds two gallons of shampoo, which is dispensed at the desired ratio with a spray gun applicator that penetrates even the thickest coat.

Omaha Vaccine's Best Care Catalog (Omaha Vaccine Co.) is a storehouse of pet-care products available through mail order. The company carries a wide selection of popular products and issues an annual catalog.

Bug X® and **One-Coat No-Bug®** (Barrier Coatings, Inc.) are antiinsect interior/exterior latex coatings that contain the insecticide chlorpyrifos. According to the manufacturer this product will kill most flying or crawling insects for more than two years following application.

Spectracide 10, Bio-Solv-C, Solv-XL and **Determed** (Bio Med Labs) are effective environmental sanitization products that help reduce the

Quick Release Leash

Skitty Witty® Feline Domicile. The optional waterbed is shown on top.

Inside view: (1) entrance, (2) food and water bowls, (3) filter, fan and light, (4) food storage area, (5) litter box, (6) carpeted floor.

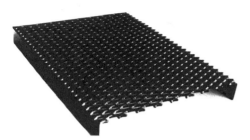

Racs Plastic Coated Animal Platforms

Easythru® Pet Doors

Chemilizer® Q-2 Quaterinary Ammonia and/or Chlorine Dispenser attaches to a regular garden hose and dispenses disinfectants.

Kennel Shade®

potential for cross-contamination from environmental surfaces in kennels and veterinary hospitals.

Racs Plastic Coated Animal Platforms (Ridglan Animal Care Systems) are heavy-duty, plastic-coated steel mesh cage racks and/or run platforms that can be incorporated in numerous ways, such as keeping coated breeds clean following grooming or prior to important dog shows.

The **Latch-Trap Spring** (Chicago Spring Co.) is a simple security device that attaches to your regular gate latch, making it virtually impossible for dogs to escape from their runs. Selling for about one dollar each, there should be one on all inside and outside pens.

Easythru® **Pet Doors** (E.G. Milligan & Co.) are a great way to allow inside/outside access to pets. They can be installed in walls, windows or glazed or penelled doors.

Kennel Shade® (Kennel Kare, Inc.) keeps dogs and cats cool on sunny days by providing a 70 percent shade factor. It also helps prevent certain coat colors from fading. A knitted monofilament, Kennel Shade is reportedly 15 time stronger than woven cloth, can withstand hail and heavy winds, does not trap water and makes an effective insect barrier. The **Kennel Kleen®** kennel disinfectant system uses a high-flow wash gun and disinfectant concentrate to clean and sanitize runs.

Farnam Pet Products (Farnam Companies, Inc.) are a complete line of new technology flea and tick control products, including collars, sprays, powders and concentrates.

Grannick's Bitter Apple® (Valhar Chemical Corp.) is a variety of taste deterrent products, including furniture cream, shampoo and plant spray that helps inhibit indiscriminate destructive chewing and self-mutilation.

De-flea (Safe and Sure Pest Kill Co.) is a nontoxic flea and tick concentrate that the manufacturer claims is totally safe for dogs, cats, kittens, puppies, nursing mothers and pregnant bitches. It contains no cholinesterase inhibitor or other poisons.

The **American Water Broom®** (American Water Broom) is a quick and easy way to clean runs, driveways and most other nonporous surfaces. The water broom produces a three-foot wide high-pressure blast of water that removes dirt and debris with minimum physical effort, while reducing the amount of water normally required for cleaning by 50 percent or more.

Spraymaster® **Automatic Insect Control** and **Portable Insect Control** (Chem-I-Matic, Inc.) mists water-based pyranha insecticide at a preset schedule to kill existing insects and inhibit reinfestation. The systems may be leased or purchased.

Dog-O-Dontics® (Canine Dental Health) are specially treated tooth-cleaning gauze pads designed to help keep a pet's teeth clean and breath fresh. The pads inhibit plaque and tartar build-up. The company also plans to develop a new line of tooth scalers designed especially for pets.

Kalglo® **Infrared (Radiant) Overhead Space Heaters** (Kalglo Elec-

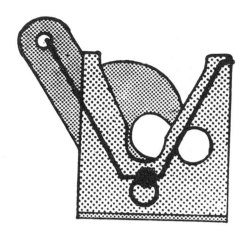

Latch-Trap Spring

American Water Broom®

Left: Spraymaster® Automatic Insect Control. Right: Spraymaster® Portable Insect Control.

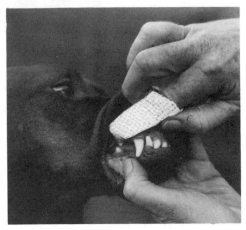

Dog-O-Dontics®

A Suburban Surgical water or feed bowl, a bowl holder attachable to both wire and chain-link fences, a cage-card holder and floor racks.

Suburban Surgical stainless steel cages.

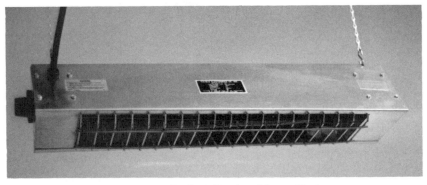

Kalglo® Infrared (Radiant) Overhead Space Heater.

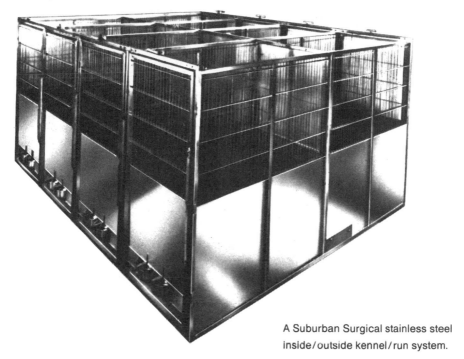

A Suburban Surgical stainless steel inside/outside kennel/run system.

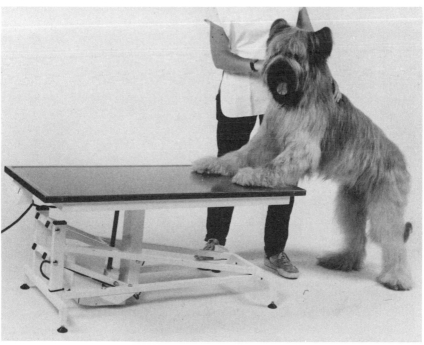

Speedy T 2000 Electric Grooming Table

203

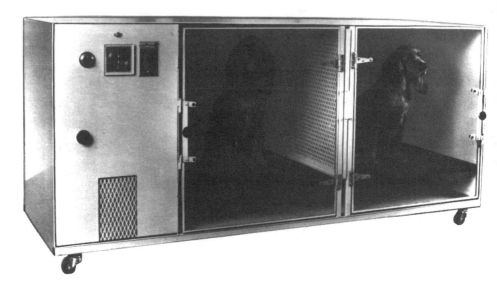

Automatic Cage Dryer

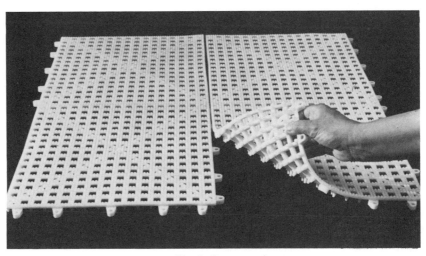

Plastic floor covering

tronics) provide an ideal solution to many kennel heating problems. They are available with solid-state temperature controls to regulate heat output and conserve energy. **Kalglo® Alarm Systems** monitor a wide variety of critical conditions including fire, power failure or unauthorized entry.

The **Nelson® Water Bucket Heater** (Nelson Manufacturing Co.) keeps the water bucket from freezing in winter—a must for all outside dogs and unheated kennels. It comes complete with an installation kit.

Spectra-Glaze II® Prefaced Concrete Masonry Units (Burns & Russell Co.) are the ultimate in custom, preglazed concrete blocks. They come in a wide variety of colors, shapes and sizes to suit every construction need.

Surburban Surgical Co., Inc. manufactures a number of quality products, including a stainless steel kennel/run system, stainless steel cages in various sizes, water and feed bowls, bowl holders (attachable to fencing), cage card holders and cage racks.

The **Speedy T 2000 Electric Grooming Table** (Rapid Electric) is a back-saver for anyone handling giant breeds. It has an extra-large work surface, elevates from 20 inches to 39 inches from the ground and plugs into any regular electrical outlet.

The **Automatic Cage Dryer** (Rea Co./Edemco) will dry dogs automatically. It is thermostatically temperature controlled for added safety. An important addition to any busy operation, it pays for itself in reduced labor costs.

Plastic floor and cage covering (Kendall Plastics, Inc.) has many useful kennel applications. It keeps animals off cold concrete and is ideal for coated breeds.

LiquidWood and **WoodEpox** (Abatron, Inc.) provide a new way to repair and regenerate weather-worn or rotted wood. This is an ideal product for upgrading existing facilities with structural damage that is difficult to replace or repair. It comes in both liquid and putty, as the names imply.

LiquidWood and WoodEpox

205

BIBLIOGRAPHY

ALL OWNERS of pure-bred dogs will benefit themselves and their dogs by enriching their knowledge of breeds and of canine care, training, breeding, psychology and other important aspects of dog management. The following list of books covers further reading recommended by judges, veterinarians, breeders, trainers and other authorities. Books may be obtained at the finer book stores and pet shops, or through Howell Book House Inc., publishers, New York.

BREED BOOKS

AFGHAN HOUND, Complete	Miller & Gilbert
AIREDALE, New Complete	Edwards
AKITA, Complete	Linderman & Funk
ALASKAN MALAMUTE, Complete	Riddle & Seeley
BASSET HOUND, New Complete	Braun
BLOODHOUND, Complete	Brey & Reed
BOXER, Complete	Denlinger
BRITTANY SPANIEL, Complete	Riddle
BULLDOG, New Complete	Hanes
BULL TERRIER, New Complete	Eberhard
CAIRN TERRIER, New Complete	Marvin
CHESAPEAKE BAY RETRIEVER, Complete	Cherry
CHIHUAHUA, Complete	Noted Authorities
COCKER SPANIEL, New	Kraeuchi
COLLIE, New	Official Publication of the Collie Club of America
DACHSHUND, The New	Meistrell
DALMATIAN, The	Treen
DOBERMAN PINSCHER, New	Walker
ENGLISH SETTER, New Complete	Tuck, Howell & Graef
ENGLISH SPRINGER SPANIEL, New	Goodall & Gasow
FOX TERRIER, New	Nedell
GERMAN SHEPHERD DOG, New Complete	Bennett
GERMAN SHORTHAIRED POINTER, New	Maxwell
GOLDEN RETRIEVER, New Complete	Fischer
GORDON SETTER, Complete	Look
GREAT DANE, New Complete	Noted Authorities
GREAT DANE, The—Dogdom's Apollo	Draper
GREAT PYRENEES, Complete	Strang & Giffin
IRISH SETTER, New Complete	Eldredge & Vanacore
IRISH WOLFHOUND, Complete	Starbuck
JACK RUSSELL TERRIER, Complete	Plummer
KEESHOND, New Complete	Cash
LABRADOR RETRIEVER, New Complete	Warwick
LHASA APSO, Complete	Herbel
MALTESE, Complete	Cutillo
MASTIFF, History and Management of the	Baxter & Hoffman
MINIATURE SCHNAUZER, New	Kiedrowski
NEWFOUNDLAND, New Complete	Chern
NORWEGIAN ELKHOUND, New Complete	Wallo
OLD ENGLISH SHEEPDOG, Complete	Mandeville
PEKINGESE, Quigley Book of	Quigley
PEMBROKE WELSH CORGI, Complete	Sargent & Harper
POODLE, New	Irick
POODLE CLIPPING AND GROOMING BOOK, Complete	Kalstone
PORTUGUESE WATER DOG, Complete	Braund & Miller
ROTTWEILER, Complete	Freeman
SAMOYED, New Complete	Ward
SCOTTISH TERRIER, New Complete	Marvin
SHETLAND SHEEPDOG, The New	Riddle
SHIH TZU, Joy of Owning	Seranne
SHIH TZU, The (English)	Dadds
SIBERIAN HUSKY, Complete	Demidoff
TERRIERS, The Book of All	Marvin
WEIMARANER, Guide to the	Burgoin
WEST HIGHLAND WHITE TERRIER, Complete	Marvin
WHIPPET, Complete	Pegram
YORKSHIRE TERRIER, Complete	Gordon & Bennett

BREEDING

ART OF BREEDING BETTER DOGS, New	Onstott
BREEDING YOUR OWN SHOW DOG	Seranne
HOW TO BREED DOGS	Whitney
HOW PUPPIES ARE BORN	Prine
INHERITANCE OF COAT COLOR IN DOGS	Little

CARE AND TRAINING

BEYOND BASIC DOG TRAINING	Bauman
COUNSELING DOG OWNERS, Evans Guide for	Evans
DOG OBEDIENCE, Complete Book of	Saunders
NOVICE, OPEN AND UTILITY COURSES	Saunders
DOG CARE AND TRAINING FOR BOYS AND GIRLS	Saunders
DOG NUTRITION, Collins Guide to	Collins
DOG TRAINING FOR KIDS	Benjamin
DOG TRAINING, Koehler Method of	Koehler
DOG TRAINING Made Easy	Tucker
GO FIND! Training Your Dog to Track	Davis
GROOMING DOGS FOR PROFIT	Gold
GUARD DOG TRAINING, Koehler Method of	Koehler
MOTHER KNOWS BEST—The Natural Way to Train Your Dog	Benjamin
OPEN OBEDIENCE FOR RING, HOME AND FIELD, Koehler Method of	Koehler
STONE GUIDE TO DOG GROOMING FOR ALL BREEDS	Stone
SUCCESSFUL DOG TRAINING, The Pearsall Guide to	Pearsall
TEACHING DOG OBEDIENCE CLASSES—Manual for Instructors	Volhard & Fisher
TOY DOGS, Kalstone Guide to Grooming All	Kalstone
TRAINING THE RETRIEVER	Kersley
TRAINING TRACKING DOGS, Koehler Method of	Koehler
TRAINING YOUR DOG—Step by Step Manual	Volhard & Fisher
TRAINING YOUR DOG TO WIN OBEDIENCE TITLES	Morsell
TRAIN YOUR OWN GUN DOG, How to	Goodall
UTILITY DOG TRAINING, Koehler Method of	Koehler
VETERINARY HANDBOOK, Dog Owner's Home	Carlson & Giffin

GENERAL

A DOG'S LIFE	Burton & Allaby
AMERICAN KENNEL CLUB 1884-1984—A Source Book	American Kennel Club
CANINE TERMINOLOGY	Spira
COMPLETE DOG BOOK, The	Official Publication of American Kennel Club
DOG IN ACTION, The	Lyon
DOG BEHAVIOR, New Knowledge of	Pfaffenberger
DOG JUDGE'S HANDBOOK	Tietjen
DOG PSYCHOLOGY	Whitney
DOGSTEPS, The New	Elliott
DOG TRICKS	Haggerty & Benjamin
EYES THAT LEAD—Story of Guide Dogs for the Blind	Tucker
FRIEND TO FRIEND—Dogs That Help Mankind	Schwartz
FROM RICHES TO BITCHES	Shattuck
HAPPY DOG/HAPPY OWNER	Siegal
IN STITCHES OVER BITCHES	Shattuck
JUNIOR SHOWMANSHIP HANDBOOK	Brown & Mason
OUR PUPPY'S BABY BOOK (blue or pink)	
SUCCESSFUL DOG SHOWING, Forsyth Guide to	Forsyth
WHY DOES YOUR DOG DO THAT?	Bergman
WILD DOGS in Life and Legend	Riddle
WORLD OF SLED DOGS, From Siberia to Sport Racing	Coppinger